PLAYING
THE GAME

PLAYING
THE GAME

A Psychopolitical Strategy
for Your Career

RAYMOND BLANK

WILLIAM MORROW AND COMPANY, INC.
New York   1981

Library of Congress Cataloging in Publication Data

Blank, Raymond.
  Playing the game.

    1. Vocational guidance—Psychological aspects.
  2. Interpersonal relations.   3. Organizational behavior.
  4. Success.   I. Title.
  HF5381.B46   650.1   80-27466
  ISBN 0-688-00354-0

Printed in the United States of America

First Edition

1 2 3 4 5 6 7 8 9 10

BOOK DESIGN BY MICHAEL MAUCERI

To my late brother Morton

and to

BARBARA
ALVIN
ADAM
JAMIE
PAUL
AND PETER

Acknowledgments

Numerous people were helpful to me during the time that I worked on this manuscript.

Special acknowledgments are due to those who offered ideas and concepts pertinent to the development of the book and to those who read and criticized all or part of the manuscript. They include Dr. Eduard Ascher, Alvin Blank, Henry Burke, and Larry Wolf and Nancy Foster-Wolf, who at an important time gave valuable criticism.

I am indebted to those who helped me in the physical preparation of the book: Deborah Reich; Paul Deegan, who gave valuable assistance in constructing the initial drafts; Carolyn Long, an extremely competent and industrious editor; Barbara Campfield; and Gail Stewart and Dana Wood, who transcribed and typed.

I would like to recognize the following people who had an exceptionally positive impact on me: Robert Bonham, president of Conversions, Inc.; Mathias DeVito, president of The Rouse Company; and Dr. Harry Levinson, president of the Levinson Institute and lecturer at the Harvard Medical School.

Finally, a special note of appreciation goes to Carol Ostrow, who insisted that this book be written, and to the late Thorpe Nesbit and his wife Elizabeth, in whose Maryland-Chesapeake Bay-Eastern Shore house much of the manuscript evolved.

—RAYMOND BLANK

Baltimore, Maryland
October, 1980

Contents

PROLOGUE. Congratulations, You're Fired! . 13

PART ONE. DECIDING TO LEAD . . . 21

CHAPTER 1. The Real Goal of Organizations . 23

CHAPTER 2. Logical Skills: Establishing Your
Base 32

CHAPTER 3. Political Skills: Creating a Career
Game Plan 42

PART TWO. HOW TO LEAD SUPERIORS . 59

CHAPTER 4. Loyalty 61

CHAPTER 5. Giving Your Boss the Credit . . 79

PART THREE. HOW TO LEAD SUBORDI-
NATES 95

CHAPTER 6. Organizations Are Like Families . 97

CHAPTER 7. Be a Good Role Model . . . 110

CHAPTER 8. The Law of Relativity 118

PART FOUR. HOW TO LEAD PEERS . . 135

CHAPTER 9. Knowing What They Want and
Getting It for Them . . . 137

PART FIVE. SOME GENERAL POLITICAL
TOOLS 161

CHAPTER 10. When to Talk 163

CHAPTER 11. When to Listen 179

CHAPTER 12. When to Put It in Writing . . . 201

SUMMARY. 212

PLAYING
THE GAME

Prologue. CONGRATULATIONS, YOU'RE FIRED!

Doing your job well may not get you promoted; in fact, it may get you fired.

Are you shocked? Are you thinking, "Is he really saying that doing good work can stunt my career, possibly even cost me my job?"

Yes, I am.

Early in 1980, CBS-TV finally recaptured the top spot in the Nielsen ratings under the leadership of its new president, John D. Backe. He was promptly fired by the chairman of the board. "On the basis of performance there seemed no reason to fire him," according to *Newsweek* magazine. Speculation held that an argument with the chairman precipitated Backe's dismissal.

This incident reflects a common fact of organizational life: No one is immune—*at any level*—from being fired for reasons unrelated to job performance.

The purpose of this book is to explain how you can avoid being trapped in your present job—or even discharged—for diligent work. *What you learn will enable you to direct the course of your career.*

In more than thirty years of consulting and working in organizations, I have observed that the career growth and salaries of the *majority of superior workers* do not reflect their levels of performance. These high performers have an inordinate number of problems at work and are often released regardless of their accomplishments. Viewing the loss of such excellent and highly productive people from business and industry convinced me that logical skills are insufficient for career success.

The opinions—and the careers—of successful people in industry, education, and government almost unanimously support these findings, as well as the explanation that gradually emerged: The men and women who operate most successfully are skilled *politically.*

Politics as defined in most dictionaries has a broad and a narrow meaning. The broad definition covers "the art or science of government." Only in a narrow sense does it connote "artful and often dishonest practices" (*Webster's Third New International Dictionary of the English Language,* 1976). The truly successful business people are skilled in the art of leading and governing.

Lynn D. Salvage, former head of the First Women's Bank of New York and now head of the Katherine Gibbs School, is such a leader. Her formula for becoming a young chief executive is described in a March 30, 1980, *New York Times* article: *"Success depends on more than just hard work, good luck and good management. Managing internal politics is very important. That aspect of business doesn't get much attention."*

The organizations with which I have consulted or worked have ranged from two-man entrepreneurships to multibillion-dollar international conglomerates; from small municipal departments to agencies as large as the United States Department of State. Even with this breadth of experience, I can recall only rare cases in which people lacking political skills did not underachieve in their careers. Their logical, classic management skills alone did not enable them to achieve rewards and recognition commensurate with their abilities.

Logical management skills aim at the creation of a product or the delivery of a service. Political skills focus on the relationships among the individuals involved in creating the product or delivering the service.

Political skills are essentially leadership skills, and you can learn them. Failure to do so can incur the loss of joy and comfort in your working life, emotional and physical health, opportunities to challenge your talent or advance your career, or even your job itself.

In contrast, becoming a politically skilled leader enables you to bring beauty, excellence, and joy to your working efforts, and generally renders appropriate financial rewards as well. It does not diminish the need for logical management skills, and the old saw, "It's not what you know; it's who you know," can be deceptive. Good management skills and logical skills are necessary but not sufficient to produce success in one's career.

The need for political skills decreases somewhat the lower one is within the organization, but it never disappears. Accordingly, the higher the performance level of an individual, the more chance he has of being fired if he lacks political skills.

An extremely competent and bright young department head was recently asked by his superior, the division head, to develop a proposal for the reorganization of the entire division. This rising star seized the opportunity to display his talents. He studied the organization of other companies in the field, enlisted professional help, and quickly produced an outstanding reorganization plan and a program for retraining those whose positions would be restructured.

The quality of this proposal far exceeded the superior's expectations and own level of management competence. The subordinate was rewarded for his efforts by a deterioration of his relationship with his boss, and ultimately was requested to leave the company under the pretext of "a division budget cut." This talented department head had become a threat to his superior, who could see the young man usurping his throne. In an effort to halt the dissolution of this relationship, the subordinate had worked even longer hours trying to please his boss.

This scenario is common. Good performers who lack political skills find their prestige declining and do the only thing they know: They work harder and perform better, which only accelerates their descent. Political skills are the "grease" an employee needs to function without causing enormous friction within an organization.

THE SEARCH FOR LEADERS

A search committee is a group appointed by a board of directors to find a potential high-level employee who has a talent the organization needs. In America today there are probably 4,000 search committees meeting in solemn conclave. The emergence of these committees in business and industry is enigmatic. Has no executive been groomed as a successor? Did the chief executive bury the brilliant and dissuade the ambitious? Did he surround himself with yesmen, who wouldn't know how to make an independent decision?

The same situation exists in the academic community. Although there are notable exceptions, colleges and universities seem inexorably drawn to the formation of search committees when they lose a chancellor or president. This may be partly explained by the fact that many brilliant professors and academics who might assume the top job successfully also have tenure. Tenure encourages creativity, eccentricity, and occasional arrogance, but it doesn't inspire the lucky ones possessing it to develop political skills. They need not warm up to their superiors, their peers, or the civilian board of trustees or directors to retain their positions.

The same explanation accounts for search committees in

17

the business world. The logically qualified candidates for promotion—those already in place and well-trained—too often lack the political acumen needed to assume leadership within their organizations. Such leadership demands a healthy balance between logical (performance) skills and political (interaction) skills.

Few people even know what *political skills* are, let alone attribute virtue to their acquisition. As with most things people don't understand, they dislike and reject them. Many excellent workers whose careers are not going well—or who are on the road to being fired—are heard saying, "I don't like to play politics."

Like it or not, we are all in the game! But those who've ignored the game all along are unlikely to know how to play effectively even if they decide to try.

You might be thinking, "I've been doing okay so far; I must be doing something right." You are surely doing *some* things right. Certain political skills evolve naturally from everyday experiences. But you may also be doing something wrong. You may not be doing those things that could substantially improve the quality of your work life. You may not be getting the just rewards your efforts deserve. If you are not, learning these skills may be the solution.

In spite of the raft of texts and how-to books on apparently similar themes, the political leadership skills required for advancement in the business world remain a mystery to most people. Many exempt themselves from the contest by saying they're just not good at politics; in reality, they've never had the opportunity to learn. The general lack of understanding of political leadership skills is evident by the increasing number of people who are disenchanted with working in organizations, opting out of large corporations, seeking a shorter work week. Absenteeism is up and productivity is down. Most of these people aren't lazy; they are deeply frustrated at their inability to maneuver in organizational life in a healthy and satisfying way.

ETHICS IN OFFICE POLITICS

The difficulty many people have in learning to lead with political skills lies in overcoming negative associations regarding "politics," which they equate with corruption or hitting below the belt. Many books exhorting the reader to be more ruthless and more manipulative than the next fellow have only reinforced a general reluctance to confront political reality. Their fear of accusations of manipulativeness and the resulting pangs of conscience can totally undermine effective leadership.

For many the very idea of learning political skills threatens the value structure by which they live. How can they "love thy neighbor" and distrust their coworkers—even when they deserve to be distrusted? How can they believe that "the meek shall inherit the earth" and accept the political ethic that "I will take control of this situation and lead it in the direction I choose"? Consequently, an open acceptance of political skills has been strongly repressed.

The truth is that political realism and good leadership are based on maturity; contrary to what many people think, integrity is not at stake. Most issues of ethics can be resolved justly by the mature leader without violating his conscience. It is virtually always possible to be "just" toward one's colleagues, to serve the organization well, and *still do the wise thing politically*. Yet nowhere have people been taught that political skills are appropriate to develop and use in the same manner as other management skills, and are even necessary to deal with the reality that good performance alone may be counterproductive to their careers.

The sports world provides a classic illustration. Whenever a team has an excellent, high-scoring player, other teams develop plays to stop him. High scoring in the business world involves increased wages and benefits, influence, and advancement. Players in the business game also develop game plans to stop the high scorer. If the top performer in either game lacks the support of his teammates, opposing game plans will defeat him.

If you are a high performer in an organization, you have adversaries developing opposing game plans. If you also possess strong political skills, you will have teammates supporting your endeavors. This book is your game plan for success—your strategy to rally people to support you and your goals.

The succeeding chapters march these valuable political skills out of the closet, explain them, and give them the dignity they deserve. Neither the sterile textbook approach nor the typical how-to treatment has offered the reader a tangible process for changing his or her work life for the better, without confusion, without guilt. This book explicitly describes the political aspects of organizations in a nonjudgmental, strategic, straightforward manner. It offers systematic guidelines which anyone can successfully apply to life on the job, as a civic volunteer or club member, to take control and advance within his or her world.

Part One. DECIDING TO LEAD

Chapter 1. THE REAL GOAL OF ORGANIZATIONS

> . . . Take note, take note, O World!
> To be direct and honest is not safe!
> —SHAKESPEARE, *Othello*

Shakespeare, a master at understanding human interactions, warned of the dangers of being too direct. He intimated further that logical skills *by themselves* could cause great trouble; for example, a player in *Timon of Athens* says:

> Every man has his fault, and honesty is his.

Many a well-intentioned supervisor and executive, having mastered logical management skills, naïvely assumes that if truth and honesty and know-how are on his or her side, he or she can't go wrong. This can be a disastrous assumption.

THE REAL GOAL OF EVERY ORGANIZATION

The first step in developing the political knowledge necessary for advancement within organizations is to understand their true goals. The widely held belief both in and out of the business community is that the ultimate goal of corporations is profit and that of government agencies and the educational community is the delivery of services.

This is not true! A deeper look at all types of organizations reveals a very different objective. The real and universal goal is *survival*. *Profit* and/or *service*, the purported goals of an organization, are really pseudo-goals, whereas *survival*—a term more taboo than sex or greed—is the fundamental goal of all. The goal of survival is neither wrong nor evil; rather, it is the most natural one for both individuals and corporations.

Profit is not the lifeblood of corporations as is often stated; it is just a life *sign*. Profit-making organizations are not primarily concerned with whether they make a profit, create a decent product, or pollute the environment. The fact of greatest importance to each member of the company is his or her weekly paycheck.

Corporations *are* looking for people to develop new products, deliver services, eliminate pollution, and give a reasonable return on investment—but never at real risk to the company. A manager who successfully performs these positive acts, which then somehow jeopardize the organization's survival, is considered irresponsible and will be forever banished from possible leadership.

The administrators of a government agency forget their public service objectives when the survival of the agency is at stake. An agency or educational institution survives if it gets a budget, irrespective of the quality of its services.

The astute politician chants his organization's chorus without dropping a beat, knowing very well that nothing could be farther from the truth if the organization itself is threatened.

Learning to survive does promote a continual search for ways to make a profit or get a budget. This need to survive is the real force behind any new thinking, and is the basis for the development of new products, policies, and approaches. It is the source of new internal attitudes and new evaluations of competition. The key to political success is precisely this understanding that organizations and individuals are motivated by survival but profess to be driven by higher motives. No one exerts influence in an organizational realm without learning the implications of this reality. Yet only a fortunate few of those spending lifetimes within companies and other organizations ever learn it.

An example of the power of this survival instinct is found in the history of the March of Dimes organization, which was created to discover a cure for polio. When the Salk vaccine against polio was developed, a huge political battle took place within the organization. Horror stories emerged detailing efforts by the March of Dimes to suppress information about the discovery of this potential miracle drug—ostensibly because there had been insufficient human testing to determine long-range effects. Actually, the discovery of the vaccine threatened the survival of the organization.

Finally, after much infighting, the vaccine was released. The organization, by then a full-grown institution, did not disappear when its *raison d'être* was eliminated. All those people who had so unstintingly given time and effort to find a polio vaccine suddenly discovered that birth defects afforded a worthy and seriously neglected cause.

Similar examples are found in government agencies and committees which continue to operate when the purpose for their creation has disappeared. When have you ever heard of a government agency going out of existence because the goals for which it was established have been accomplished?

Zero-base budgeting, designed to halt the growth of uncontrolled government bureaucracy, was heralded much as the coming of the Messiah. Under this system, the budget petitioner must prove the merit of the endeavor as if there were no previous budget. This Messiah is looking less and less as if it will perform any miracles.

And in the private sector, when have you ever seen a company *willingly* close its doors and distribute its assets to its stockholders when it could no longer make a profit? Almost never. Organizations, like people and other living things, will do almost anything to satisfy the will to survive.

The need for political skills stems from this dichotomy

between a company's stated goals and its real, unstated survival goal. Just as success is sure to elude the employee working industriously toward the company's stated goals if he is oblivious to the real one, so open recognition of the real goal does not generate any laurels, as such revelation may bring vulnerability to the company. The politically astute understand that the real goal is survival—but never speak of it.

The merits of openness and honesty were the focus of a thirteen-week management seminar on logical skills once offered by a leading business college. A survey one year later revealed that over half the graduates of the seminar had left their jobs. Follow-up interviews disclosed that their application of those management skills had generated serious conflicts for the graduates within their organizations.

While the logical and honest observation may be directly on target, it can also successfully undermine a friendship, marriage, deal, promotion, or job. An individual skilled only in the logical "horse-sense" skills of management seems to be wearing blinkers which prevent his seeing the other horses in the race for the roses of success. His firmly fixed goal is the finish line, and he streaks alone, oblivious to his competition. He is unaware of and unconcerned with the direct bumps he gives them or the honest dust and mud he kicks up in his wake. But the ignominy of their defeats in the trial heats is not soon forgotten, and his competitors may very well pin him to the rail in later and more important encounters.

The logically direct and honest businessman is, for the most part, threatening to those around him. Such an executive exposes his unprotected flanks to those who curry the favor of *his* superiors by relating eerie tales of the *logical* maverick. His competitors—all too aware of their own imperfections—may resent a similar awareness on his part. If any colleague harbors secret fears that he is uncultured, cheap, boorish, stupid, or biased, a hint that someone else knows of his clay feet and may point them out "in all honesty" could turn him into a rampaging avenger.

The direct and logical person who adds *political skills* to his talents may achieve his desired ends without spilling blood or ending up on someone's "enemies list."

PRESERVING THE IMAGE

The executive who deals only in "truth and honesty"—that is, "Only the facts, Ma'am"—may be unaware of the importance most people put on the preservation of a personal image. "Image" in this case is not necessarily a reflection of reality; it is the slightly warped reflection of how an individual feels he looks and should be viewed by his peers, superiors, and subordinates. An honest, direct, or logical judgment of someone may not distort reality, but it may destroy his "image." Most superiors and peers don't require an infallible mirror; they have already reached the unsupported conclusion that they are the best in the game.

A superior's self-image may be that he is kind, compassionate, underpaid, an expert in his field, responsible for the success of his company, and that by his personal magnetism he has attracted the orders that provide work and income for his subordinates. This image may differ greatly from the shattered reflection seen by the logical and honest underling who learns that his boss wouldn't know a magnifying glass from the sophisticated scanner which his company manufactures; that he overruled marketing three times before he found that billion-dollar market out there; and that his alcoholism and vulgarity have driven away a significant volume of orders.

Each of us, of course, has a self-image we protect. We resent those who tell us a disturbing truth, or invoke an unarguable logic, or speak with innocent directness.

Few superiors, in fact probably none, really want to hear

an employee's idea of the complete truth about them and their ideas. With little coaxing, most would confess they agree with Mark Twain's assertion, "I like criticism, but it must be my way." Tempted though you may be to tell the emperor he has no clothes, be alerted that he is more likely to perceive your observations as disloyalty than as constructive criticism.

One day you may be having a friendly conversation with your boss over a few drinks at the High Noon Bar and Cafeteria, when he suddenly asks you what you *really* think of him as a boss.

"Oh," you'll probably say, "I think you're great, Mr. Blivens." Suppose he persists.

"Tell me *honestly*," he cajoles. "Don't be afraid! I want the truth!"

Don't you believe it! Many a promising career was ruined when a subordinate ventured to blurt out his deep-seated annoyance with some of his boss's work habits.

"Thanks a bunch," the Boss might say. "I appreciate your telling me that. In the future, I'll try to read all your memos and respond more quickly."

He may not pay you back right away for the embarrassment, but he will at the appropriate time. Regardless of the words he mouths, he is hungry to hear that he is a great boss without even minor flaws. Of course, a competent and well-adjusted manager shouldn't mind hearing your honest opinion of him or her, particularly since it's likely to be mostly positive. Such a person would incorporate your constructive observations to become an even better executive. But how many subordinates have a boss who is all that competent and well adjusted?

Equally damaging to a subordinate's relationship with a superior is an unflattering comment on the superior's recent speech, office decor, staff, secretary, car, dog, bridge or golf game, religious preference, sexual preference, brand of

Scotch, favored political candidate, or fit of summer slacks. For if, in honest response to a superior's request for an opinion about any of the above, you betray even the slightest disapproval of his or her taste, you have taken a giant step on the path to being fired.

For the most part, your superiors and your peers don't want logic and honesty and directness from you. They want the recognition and respect their self-images command. The image may be a dream world, but they want no intrusions on what they have convinced themselves is reality.

Exalted strains of the Egalitarian Anthem ring out from the offices of managers throughout the country. Proudly they proclaim their allegiance to democracy in the workplace and their longing for truth. Effusively they cite their egalitarian practices. Yet a rare bird is the manager who actually maintains any form of honest and democratic environment. While the general chorus of a company or agency loudly chants its nonauthoritarianism, most superiors, practicing in solo, are too insecure to allow real participation by subordinates, particularly if that participation takes the form of criticism.

If you believe that a company or an agency is a democracy, you probably also believe that the Indians were happy with the Manhattan Island transfer, or that the South has forgotten the Civil War. Yet at departmental dinners and picnics and awards banquets, some general managers—influenced by the martinis and the comradery—are inclined to tell the assemblage that "this is a democratic organization and my door is always open."

Don't let that "open door" fool you either! Unless you are clutching in your hand an unexpected five-million-dollar order, four box-seat tickets for the World Series, a complimentary article about the Boss in *Forbes*, or his final divorce papers, don't expect to be greeted by anything other than boredom, distrust, and annoyance as you stroll into your superior's office.

Obsessive honesty about the faults of the organization is just as dangerous as total honesty with your boss about his or her faults. Pointing out the company's faults is called "not singing the Company Song."

Those who hope to advance in organizational life must learn to sing the organizational song whether or not they believe it. The aspiring corporate executive masters such idioms as:

"We at Bull Manufacturing believe in a free market. We feel that we have a public duty not to pollute the environment while we give our stockholders a reasonable return on their investment through the generation of profits. We feel a public duty to deliver an excellent product to the consumer at a reasonable price."

The government agency overture sounds like:

"We at the Bull Conservation Department exist to deliver a service. Our goal is to deliver that service to the taxpayers at the most reasonable cost."

Public agencies claim to have an open-door policy in compliance with the recently passed Freedom of Information Act and "sunshine laws," but employees as well as heads of federal agencies invariably reverberate the "agency line":

"Our agency is convinced that the public has a right to know exactly what's going on in government. We here in the Desultory Depository Department have absolutely nothing to hide. Our meetings always have minutes, and we welcome public access to those minutes as well as to other communications." The reality is that in almost all cases the agency would like to hold its meetings behind closed doors. They would like to have all their written communications classified as "top secret" in the interest of national security.

Most managers in the private sector and their public agency counterparts believe theoretically in an open-door policy, public access to information, and democracy in the workplace; but when it comes down to a specific meeting or situation, the cry is, *"We should treat this matter on a 'need-to-know' basis."*

With such disparity between the *stated* goals and policies of an organization and its *actual* goals and practices, one must cultivate political skills to survive. Direct and honest logic works only in an open and honest environment, which rarely exists in today's work world.

Chapter 2. LOGICAL SKILLS: ESTABLISHING YOUR BASE

A fundamental principle of this book is that you cannot succeed in organizations and companies by using *only* logical skills. Success depends on both *logical* and *political* skills. Political skills alone may enable you to maneuver for a time, but without a solid base of logical skills and good performance, you'll be a flash in the pan.

Effective use of political skills, then, is contingent on the development of logical skills. Hundreds of books have evaluated these logical management tools, so this book is not intended to be a comprehensive study of them. Rather, it provides a brief explanation of each of the five major areas of logical skills to emphasize their importance as a foundation for all management development.

The *five basic logical skills* for successful management are:

    I.   *Structure*
   II.   *Participation*
 III.   *Goal Setting*
 IV.   *Time Management*
  V.   *Decision Making and Problem Solving*

The Managerial Diamond (see diagram at end of chapter) provides a model for a management system incorporating these skills. Proper application of the Managerial Diamond results in an effective, performance-oriented organization. It generates a "brick" orientation; that is, every task has a clear purpose and a tangible result. It produces a "brick" that clearly fits into the larger organizational structure and program.

The first of the five basic logical tools for the successful management of organizations is:

I. STRUCTURE

Just as a good financial manager has a clean balance sheet, a good human resources manager has a clean structure.

A. *A clean structure reflects reality.*

No phantom figures with high-sounding titles belong on the organizational chart. An "unclean" structure is usually the result of a company's fear of admitting that a once powerful executive has become a director with no staff to direct or a manager with nothing to manage. The superior in this case may be too compassionate to hurt the feelings of his or her coworker by advertising to the small world of the company that the phantom's wings have been clipped and his former clout redistributed.

Kicks upstairs, downstairs, and sideways should not be inaccurately illustrated on an organizational chart. Otherwise titles don't mean anything, and nobody is sure what the power structure really is. Personal feelings are never long assuaged in such an "unclean" structure; those whose power in the palace has been diminished are well aware of the fact.

B. *A clean structure is one in which each person has only one boss.*

A high-performance worker with more than one boss will become frustrated trying to determine whom to obey. A malingerer reporting to more than one person can easily hide his or her lack of productivity. An employee working for more than one person doesn't really work for anyone.

Under a matrix structure an individual may perform duties for several areas of the company and while working for each department, may officially report to that department. An employee working for more than one department could have any number of bosses. This type of avant-garde structure may be necessary and desirable under certain circumstances, but in the main, an individual should not be asked to wear many hats or serve multiple masters.

Straight lines on an organizational chart show who reports to whom. Dotted lines generally represent an indefinite reporting relationship. Undefined reporting connections are almost always ineffective and should therefore be avoided. Clean structures do not have dotted lines.·

C. *A clean structure is one that avoids "one on one."*

The term may conjure up an exciting basketball situation in which the players clear out the lanes and Dr. J. or "Magic" Johnson or Darrell Griffiths goes "one on one" against a single defender.

In business jargon the term refers to a supervisor or executive who has only one other human being reporting to him or her. This is a sure sign that either the superior or subordinate is redundant. The two will soon be battling or scheming to point the finger at the one who is not needed.

D *To attain a clean structure, a good manager remembers five vital rules.*

1. The good manager puts his or her best workers on the line and the strong thinkers with people skills in staff positions. He or she is aware that line jobs produce the service or product and that the staff supports the line.

2. The good manager allows individuals to grow by letting them take on new duties and responsibilities, thus enriching their jobs without necessarily restructuring the organization.

3. The good, logically skilled manager avoids the temptation of promoting his best worker to the head of a department when he knows the individual would be a questionable manager. He thereby avoids losing his best worker to gain a poorly managed department. (Player-managers usually don't pan out in sports or in business.)

4. The good manager does not allow himself or anyone within the organization to exceed the *span of control*; i.e., no one has more people reporting to him than he can adequately and competently supervise.

A sure sign that he has exceeded the span of control is that he finds it impossible to meet individually with those he supervises for at least one or two hours a week.

5. A good manager is prepared to commit to writing and graphics his organizational structure. In this way there is no doubt about what is going on, who reports to whom, and who is in charge of what.

The second of the five basic logical tools for the successful management of organizations is:

II. PARTICIPATION

Once a manager has a clean and well-organized structure, he or she should focus attention on developing a healthy participative environment. Anyone within such a structure will perform at or near his optimum.

The manager of a healthy participative environment:

A. *Promotes Teamwork*

The teamwork spirit flows from the manager. A team is a group of people with a leader, but in the area of ideas *everyone is equal.* An idea is not per se better because it was born in the mind of the manager.

The effective leader achieves his or her goals not by demanding compliance to orders or by bribing subordinates, but by creating an atmosphere in which everyone feels he is a part of an effective, well-organized team.

B. *Utilizes Conflict*

A good team leader promotes a healthy conflict of ideas and views among subordinates. This type of leader realizes that conflict enriches the soil in which creativity flourishes.

Authoritarian as well as Nice Guy environments should be avoided:

In an *authoritarian* environment, *conflict is suppressed* by prohibition. Managers are taught that there is only one way to do a job or view a situation, and they are brainwashed by company or corporate philosophy to ignore even the most persuasive arguments of their subordinates.

In a *Nice Guy* environment, the soft-style manager wants everyone to love him. He doesn't want conflict of any kind. He smooths everything over. He tries to lead by being liked. He has a friendly enough company, *but with low production*. His product, his "brick," is more like an egg.

The manager in a healthy participative environment gives employees what they really want: experience on a tough team; the *opportunity to participate* in the resolution of conflict; the *challenge of an important job*; the *feeling of achievement*; *responsibility*; and the *chance for growth, advancement, and recognition*.

The third of the five basic logical skills or tools for the successful management of organizations is:

III. GOAL SETTING

Both the organization and the individual employee must have measurable and attainable goals. If a goal is unattainable it is not a goal—it is a dream. *The company must have its goals, and the goals of its employees must contribute to the attainment of the company goals.*

Effective company goal setting is *imaginative as well as realistic*, and includes the inherent directive of striving *to exceed its goals*. Constant and honest communications among all elements of the company—financial, engineering, production, marketing, personnel—assure that nothing slips through the cracks.

Only when a performance review of an individual's goals is done on a periodic basis can it ensure the attainment of the company goals. A useful performance review or appraisal is a formal discussion between superior and subordinate, at scheduled times and set intervals. The subordinate should leave the sessions knowing how he or she is doing and equipped with some ideas for improvement.

Once a manager has achieved a *clean structure*, operating within a *healthy participative environment*, and an organization which has—along with its employees—*attainable and measurable goals*, he works on the acquisition of *time management skills*, the fourth of the five basic logical tools necessary for the effective management of organizations:

IV. TIME MANAGEMENT

The following illustration represents the difficulties some people have managing their valuable time.

There are twenty-four hours in every day. You sleep seven hours; that leaves seventeen. Meals take two hours; that leaves fifteen. Dressing and aspects of personal care take an hour; that leaves fourteen. Travel to and from work takes an hour and a half; that leaves twelve and a half. Reading the newspapers, magazines, and books takes an hour; that leaves eleven and a half. Recreation of one form or the other takes an hour (longer on weekends); that leaves ten and a half. Television takes an hour. Family matters take one and a half hours. That leaves eight hours.

You now have a precious eight hours left to do a good day's work, to be creative and productive. For most people this doesn't happen. The last eight hours are more often spent in the following fashion:

On the telephone, one hour; batting the verbal ball with coworkers, half an hour; daydreaming about fishing, flying, flirting, or whatever, half an hour; attending unnecessary and senseless meetings, one hour; composing detailed memorandums or imaginative expense accounts, one hour; walking to and from meetings, half an hour; shopping, one hour; and mentally solving the bigger problems of the world, one hour. This leaves one and a half hours for honest-to-goodness work.

I might have exaggerated a bit, but not much. Time is valuable and must be managed.

The major time management skill is that of *setting priorities.* There isn't time to accomplish everything, so a good manager chooses what's necessary and lets everything else wait.

Having determined the things he should accomplish on a priority basis, the good manager takes control of the four ways people typically interrupt him which prevent his doing the things he has prioritized:

A.   They drop in unannounced.

B.   They call him to meetings at which his presence is not necessary. The meetings themselves may not be necessary.

C.   They telephone, and the nonsense syllables outnumber the sensible five to one.

D.   They send long, padded reports and memorandums.

To manage your time and utilize your talents, you must when necessary:

1.   Shut the door.
2.   Send a substitute ear to meetings.
3.   Don't take calls.
4.   Demand short memos.

Then work like mad to make your accomplishments equal your talent. You need time and should not let people take it from you.

Once the good manager has achieved a *clean structure,* is operating within a *healthy participative environment* with *goals and performance appraisals,* and is maximizing his hours through proper *time management,* he now turns his attention to the fifth logical tool for the effective management of organizations:

V. DECISION MAKING AND PROBLEM SOLVING

The making of decisions and the solving of problems require entirely different disciplines. In most business and government offices, the terms *decision* and *problem* are used interchangeably, and as a result neither decisions nor problems are handled as effectively as they might be. Yet a study done by a "think tank" in California recently revealed a high correlation between business success and the ability to solve problems and make decisions in an organized manner.

Decision making is deciding where to go: the new product, the new plant, the new plant manager, the new advertising campaign. Problem solving is finding out what happened if you decided to go, went, didn't get there at all, or didn't get there on time.

Good decision makers avoid the trap of generating alternatives ("We should move the plant to Florida or South Carolina") before listing their wants ("We should move the plant closer to our markets and to a milder climate to cut energy costs"). By generating alternatives first, one tends to slant his or her wants to suit an emotionally desirable alternative. Equal emphasis may be placed on unequal factors, and a plant which belongs near Charleston, South Carolina, may end up in Florida because one person prefers it.

Sometimes a manager picks the wrong man for a particular position, the wrong market for a product, or the wrong location for the plant. He has made a decision. If he later recognizes that he has chosen a poor alternative, he may call on his problem-solving apparatus before there is a business disaster. He finds solid answers to his first mistake before making a second decision.

Problem solving is finding out where something went

wrong. Every problem has only *one* cause at its base, hence, the law of cause and effect—not *causes* and effect. The cause is always something that changed, so the capable problem solver always looks for a change.

Answering the following questions often helps when seeking the cause of a problem.

1. Exactly what is the nature of the problem?
2. When did it start?
3. What is the geographical location of the problem?
4. Has the problem remained the same since it started?
5. If it has changed, in what way has it changed?
6. How many were affected?
7. Which ones were affected and which were not?
8. Were they all affected the same?
9. If not, what was different?
10. How much were they affected?

To verify that the cause which emerges in answer to these questions is correct, you must determine whether it coincides with the onset of the problem.

In summary, if you develop all these logical skills—*structure, participation, goal setting and performance review, time management, and decision making and problem solving*—you are on your way to business success. If you also master the *political skills*, you will most assuredly succeed.

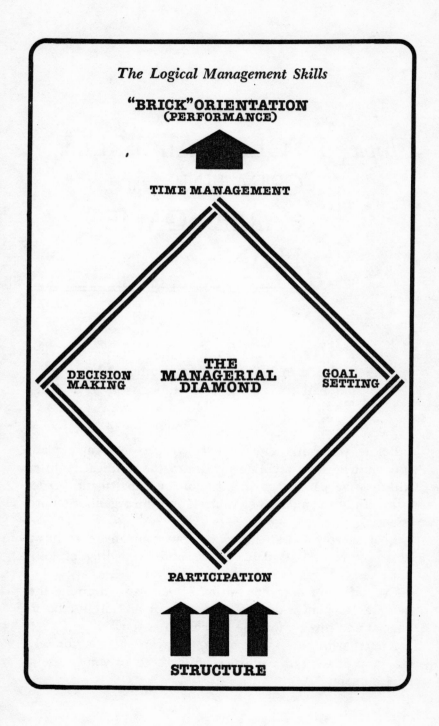

The Logical Management Skills

"BRICK"ORIENTATION
(PERFORMANCE)

TIME MANAGEMENT

DECISION
MAKING

THE
MANAGERIAL
DIAMOND

GOAL
SETTING

PARTICIPATION

STRUCTURE

Chapter 3. POLITICAL SKILLS: CREATING A CAREER GAME PLAN

If a man look sharply and attentively,
he shall see Fortune; for though she is
blind, she is not invisible . . .
—FRANCIS BACON

Before you can create an effective personal game plan, you must have an accurate picture of the political realities within your particular organization or department. A detailed study and analysis of yourself and the organization are essential.

Look sharply and attentively at your company, examining its structure and its past, future, and overriding philosophies.

Evaluate your current position so you can determine the best way to plan a desired advancement and attain the financial and psychic fortune which awaits you.

Armed with this information, you can more accurately take aim at the skills you need to succeed in your present environment.

DEVELOPING YOUR GAME PLAN

The best way to create a personal career game plan is outlined in the six steps below. (The game plan illustrated is for a public profit-making company, but the same techniques can apply to government or nonprofit organizations.)

STEP I. DETERMINE THE CHARACTERISTICS OF YOUR ORGANIZATION

Accomplish this first step in the game plan by examining such physical things as facilities, people, and products, as well as the political milieu in which these things exist.

Start by acquiring as much publicly printed matter as possible. Offices and departments right in the home office can be veritable gold mines of information. Some sources are obvious, such as the public relations office, from which you can obtain all the company's press releases and brochures.

Other sources of information are less obvious but may prove more valuable. A good example is the accounting department, where you will find such neglected and revealing documents as the company annual reports for the current year as well as for at least the last five years, plus anything the company has filed with the S.E.C. (the Securities and Exchange Commission of the federal government) if it is a public company.

Because the accounting departments of most companies feel that no one really understands—or, therefore, appreciates—what they do, your attention is likely to evoke considerable cooperation.

Deciphering the Company Annual Report

The following examination of a *Company Annual Report* illustrates the fact that many public documents reveal political information to the careful reader. These reports often appear dull at first glance, with lots of mysterious numbers and unrecognizable names. But with study and possibly some help in deciphering them, you will likely find a cornucopia of information which is not in the least boring.

The President's Letter,
or Who's Singing the Company Song

The President's Letter is almost always at the beginning of the report. This message purports to tell the stockholders what happened during the year and what will be happening in the future. Most of the letter is nothing more than propaganda, better known as the Company Song. There is, however, political value in your knowing exactly what the Company Song is. If you are ever in the presence of top management, you will find it is not unusual for them to play "Name That Tune," and if you can chime in with a few familiar bars of the Company Song, you win. However, if you can't even name the song, you'll probably elicit cold stares.

A closer examination of *The President's Letter* will often reveal the outline of the company's long-range plan. The long-range plan is supposed to be secret to avoid its possible use by the competition, so it is theoretically inaccessible to any but the top inner circle. The organization's long-range plan is invaluable as you develop your long-range career plan. It tells you which areas of the company will ultimately be in the limelight. And if you want to be a star, you'll need to know where the spotlight is going to be! Those in power in areas of intended company growth are likely to see their prestige and influence grow as well. You surely want to know who will be important in the long run.

Also hidden between the lines of *The President's Letter* will probably be the company's immediate plans to solve its most pressing problems. By comparing this short-range plan with the long-range one, you can determine which departments currently on the rise are only shooting stars, soon to burn up. Attaching oneself to a particular area, department, or person called to the forefront only to solve short-range problems is a serious tactical error. A division which is not intrinsic to the company's long-range goals will eventually decline.

An in-depth review of the dialogue in *The Annual Report* as well as *The President's Letter* may reveal who is in favor or disfavor. If you know the praised and the damned, you can avoid putting your foot in your mouth, or your career in a losing situation.

This raises the issue of whether one should stay away from an individual who has fallen into disfavor with the power base of the organization. Should you no longer associate with your old friend because the top brass doesn't like him anymore and he'll probably soon be fired? Will you be tarnished if you continue to go out to lunch with him or have drinks with him after work? The answer depends on the value of that particular relationship to you. It will surely not help your career to associate with people who are in disfavor; there will be guilt by association in the eyes of management. As a general rule, if the relationship is extremely valuable to you, then continue it; otherwise give it up.

Important Names and Numbers

In *The Annual Report* you will also find the **financial information** of the company. It is wise to acquaint yourself with this knowledge. If numbers are not your thing, ask someone you know and trust who understands something about accounting to decipher them for you. In this way you can confirm which areas or divisions are doing well and which are operating in the red. Naturally you will want to consider guiding your career to those places that are performing successfully.

The Annual Report also lists the members of the **board of directors** of the company. This is of tremendous political value. Following the board members' names are their organizational affiliations. The board of directors usually contains what are referred to as "inside" and "outside" directors. An *inside director* is either employed by or very closely related to the company. An *outside director* has little affiliation with the company besides serving on its board.

An inside director who works for the company will be pleased to hear that you noticed he or she is on the board of directors. Whenever you introduce someone who is a director, be sure to mention it: for example, "This is so and so, our Vice-President in charge of Administration, who is also a director of our company."

It is helpful for you to know who the outside directors are and the companies or government agencies with which they are connected. There is usually some form of the old "You scratch my back, I'll scratch yours" game going on. If you plan to order any kind of supplies, for instance, it behooves you to order them from a company represented on the board of directors. It certainly won't hurt your career if at a board meeting an outside director mentions to your president that you are someone with whom it's easy to do business.

Don't Skip the Fine Print

Acquainting yourself with the **footnotes** to *The Annual Report* can prove indispensable. The footnotes will point directly to the problem areas of the company. It is here that the independent auditors try to justify the term "independent" by making the company hang out its dirty linen publicly.

A case in point:

The Fortress Home Builders, in need of door frames, purchased the Easy Open Door Frame Company near the beginning of their fiscal year. Fortress had a disastrous year, but their new door-frame company had a tremendous one. This prosperity, however, was due not so much to their ongoing keen business acumen as to their good fortune in having bought a large quantity of wood the year before at a never-to-be-found-again price.

Enter *The Annual Report*. The Fortress Home Builders tells their auditors they want to print a consolidated statement of all their divisions, on the pretext that they don't want their competitors to know what they're doing. In reality, they don't want the word out that they're on the verge of bankruptcy!

A compromise is struck with the independent auditors. Fortress agrees to insert an obscure footnote regarding the purchase in *The Annual Report*, which YOU, the now-astute reader of annual reports, are able to decipher. The footnote reads:

> Note j—The Easy Open Door Frame Co. was acquired on July 20, 1980, and benefited from a favorable inventory position.

These footnotes appear, of course, in the smallest print ever devised, so be sure to bring along your glasses. You'll want to know where the company's dirty linen is kept so you won't inadvertently get any of the dirt on you.

The Annual Report also tells you the names of the **public accounting firm** that does its audit, as well as the company's **general counsel**. It is useful to know who these people are when you bump into them around the home office.

The name of the company's **primary bank** is in the report also. Banking there yourself offers certain advantages. First, it shows management your wisdom in choosing the same bank as the company did. Further, it enables you to acquaint yourself with the top brass at the bank.

Often you will find the **organizational chart** of the company in *The Annual Report*. This chart is a singularly important career-planning tool, and you will ultimately use it to determine the shortest and best route to your career destination within the organization. You will ordinarily find names within the boxes on the chart whose favor you may need along your way.

There will also be a complete list of **divisions, plants,** and any other **facilities** that your company owns and operates. This information is important for a variety of reasons. For example, you can expect at some time during your trip up the corporate ladder to be transferred into the field for seasoning, so early on, choose a division you like and cultivate friendships within that organization. In that way you will have contacts eager for you to spend your outside penance in their amicable environment.

Another reason for knowing everything the company owns is that it will probably tell you a great deal about the *origins of the organization*, which is important if the founders are still in power. Founders never seem to want to close the original plant. They like to keep it as some kind of good luck charm even though it is often inefficient and outdated. If you are going to advance, it is an extremely good idea to be able to praise the origins of the company.

As stated earlier, reading *The Annual Report* is just one way you can learn a tremendous amount about your organization in a political sense merely by looking at the materials produced for public consumption. Some other readily available documents and unlikely places in which you might find valuable material are described below.

Knowing What the S.E.C. Knows

An additional useful document found in the accounting department is *Form 10K*, which the company files with the S.E.C. Much of the same information found in *The Annual Report* appears again in *Form 10K* but in much greater depth. It will contain an analysis of the company's competition—obviously valuable material if for some reason you leave the company.

Also included is a profile on all the officers of the company. Executives generally focus on the areas they know best. You will want to know their work history because, one way or another, the limelight swings back to where they started. There is a principle that the person with the highest visibility will probably get the next promotion. You don't want to harass, but you do want the limelight—and here's a good way to find it.

This report also contains a complete list of any significant changes that took place within the company during the year. It gives a clear explanation of any profit-sharing plans, retirement benefits, and stock-option plans. It tells who is entitled to them and when.

Before leaving the accounting office, pick up any prospectuses the company has issued during the year. A prospectus gives the current financial statement required by law for any company selling stock. It may provide more current information than the *10K* form or *The Annual Report*.

Personnel Is More Than a People Placer

Another cache of intelligence is the personnel office, where you can find detailed brochures used to attract prospective employees. If there is no public relations office, it is here that you will find press releases and public relations materials.

As you continually gather information to increase your political data base, you can cross-check the pieces of data to verify their accuracy. Investigative reporters for *The Washington Post* used this method to piece together the Watergate scandal. In the same way you can piece together the inner workings of your organization.

Call Your Broker

Continue your investigation by calling a stockbroker in your community. If you already have one, so much the better; otherwise, call and say you want to talk about opening an account. In short order you will have your own stockbroker.

Your new broker has a great deal of the information we have already discussed, should you be unable to obtain it from your own company. In addition, the brokerage house has access to independent analyses of your company which provide potential investors with the knowledge to make a good decision. The material is, therefore, more unbiased.

At the brokerage office you will find another resource which can be used on an ongoing basis. Recently a computer program was instituted in most large brokerage houses around the country which gives the broker access to all national newspaper and magazine articles about a company. It prints the headline of an article on a video screen with the source and the date. If you want to read the complete article, your broker can, by pushing a few keys, produce the full text on the video screen.

A telephone call to the Securities and Exchange Commission in Washington, D.C., is another way to obtain a complete list of whatever your company files with them.

A call to your local newspaper will also prove fruitful. Their files contain clippings from their own paper as well as from many others. If the paper seems reticent to give you information, a little coaxing by you or an influential friend should make available anything the paper has on file.

Your Own Company Library

Let us assume that through your investigative methods you have amassed a substantial informational library, and have intimate knowledge of the material on your company. For easy accessibility file each important piece of data by subject matter on a three- by five-inch card. With this file operative, you are well on your way to completing Step I: determining the characteristics of your organization.

STEP II: LEARN WHAT THE ORGANIZATION AND YOUR BOSS EXPECT FROM YOU

By embarking on a series of personal interviews you can complete Step I as well as Step II, thereby learning what the organization and your boss expect of you presently and where they see your eventual role in the organization.

The interviewees might be your boss, his peers, your peers, or your subordinates. Develop a list of questions to clarify your objectives and talk to anyone you think can answer one or more of them. The following are some sample questions concerning the organization:

1. *What does top management want from me?*
2. *What does my immediate boss want from me?*
3. *Does this organization favor entrepreneurial style or formalized style?*
4. *What is the role of the personnel department?*
5. *What are the stated promotion policies?*
6. *What kinds of people really advance and get promotions in this organization?*
    a. *Does there seem to be a personality type which succeeds?*
    b. *Do they share clothing preferences?*
    c. *Do they have the same prejudices in common?*
7. *What departments are in favor?*
8. *What departments are not in favor?*
9. *Is the company's growth carefully planned or haphazard?*
10. *Are there family members of the company in the lower ranks, working their way up? Where is Will, Jr., going?*

Here are some suggested questions regarding your superior:

11. *Is my boss in the mainstream of the company?*
12. *What are his or her ambitions?*
13. *What is my boss's marital partner like?*
    a. *What is their relationship like?*
    b. *What activities do they enjoy?*
14. *What are my boss's favorite recreations?*
15. *What kind of car does he or she drive?*
16. *Does my boss drink? How much? When? With whom?*

17. What are his or her views on morality? Does he or she wear a wedding ring?

18. What kind of vacations does my boss prefer? Seaside? Mountains? Home?

19. What are the names of his or her children? What schools do they attend?

20. What are my boss's spending habits?

21. In what kind of house does he or she live? In what kind of neighborhood?

22. To what clubs does he or she belong?

23. To what charities does he or she contribute?

24. To what churches or organizations does he or she belong?

25. What are his or her political affiliations?

26. Where did my boss go to school? What did he or she study?

This information may take three or four months to compile, but it is eminently worthwhile and considerably more interesting than coffee-break gossip.

Naturally you will not take notes at these interviews, so it is important to debrief yourself as soon as the interview is over by writing down all the details you can remember. Add this to your ever-growing important fact file.

STEP III. SELF-ANALYSIS

When you have a substantial data base, you will have completed Steps I and II and can now proceed to Step III: an in-depth analysis of yourself.

The accounting sheet on yourself should contain the answers to three basic questions:

1. What am I presently doing in this organization?

2. What do I really like to do?

3. What do I really dislike doing?

Take time to answer the above questions thoughtfully and honestly and in some depth. It will do you little good to write down such superficial responses as: "I'm a little cog in a big wheel and I'd like to be the big wheel." Taken seriously, this exercise will enable you to use the political skills explained throughout this book to achieve your own career goals.

Consider these questions individually:

1. What am I presently doing in this organization?

In answering this question you are creating an accurate job description. If yours is one of the canned job descriptions supplied by the personnel department, it describes your work as something quite different than what you actually do each day.

Don't fool yourself. That job description probably evolved because someone wanted to give more—or less—salary to the job or placate someone's ego, and it therefore doesn't reflect the actual work performed. Besides that, you have probably been responsive to your boss's wishes even when they went beyond your job description.

An accurate job description, listing all your functions, is an essential ingredient in career planning. Perhaps the easiest way to be sure you have listed everything is to create a chart listing each of the jobs you do. This flow chart will be helpful later when we address goal setting as a political tool in Chapter 8.

The fresh new perspective you will gain by creating this job description will allow you to see what you are actually accomplishing within the organization, and exactly where you stand in the hierarchy.

Place the second and third questions at the top of two columns on the same sheet of paper, and answer them thoroughly.

2. What do I really like to do?
3. What do I really dislike doing?

STEP IV. DECIDE WHAT POSITION YOU ULTIMATELY WANT TO HOLD

Compare the Lists for Compatibility

Proceed slowly and thoughtfully, and when you are done, evaluate your likes and dislikes in relation to each other, as well as against your appraisal of the company, to see if this is the type of environment which suits you.

Next, compare your likes and dislikes to your real job description; if they relate favorably, you know you are suited for your job.

If the work you enjoy and the company's expectations do not correlate favorably, then you should probably think about launching a new job search. With the work you have done so far you should now be in a position to see how far along with your life goals this organization will allow you to go, and the position for which you can realistically reach.

Once you've decided on a direction, you can clearly focus on your goal. You will be aiming with the precision of a finely sighted rifle instead of the diffusion of a shotgun.

STEP V. PLAN HOW TO GET FROM WHERE YOU ARE TO WHERE YOU WANT TO GO

A. *Map your stepping-stones to success.*

Develop a list of stepping-stone jobs from the one you have to the one for which you are best suited. These jobs are essentially safehouses from which you can move easily and securely along your way.

B. *Mark the "Danger" signs on your map.*

List any jobs which could prove hazardous to your career advancement. This includes ones for which you are unsuited, as well as those which are politically unfavorable. Beware of jobs which lead you away from your goal.

C. *Chart your career map on paper.*

5

Design a step-by-step visual map which charts the jobs to be pursued and avoided on the way to your goal.

D. *Estimate the time framework.*

Include on your map the approximate time you think each step will take. Totaling the estimates for each step will give you an idea of the time necessary to get to your goal position.

E. *Note the key players.*

List members of the organization who could help your advancement at each step along the way.

The primary purpose of the remainder of this book is to show you how to influence the key players who *can* help you to *want* to do so.

A common situation is that many of the people on your list of potential supporters do not yet know you, or know you only slightly. Still others may know you well but are committed presently to your failure rather than to your success. *The skills you acquire from reading this book will enable you to turn most of these people—even your present detractors—into supporters of your endeavors.*

STEP VI. REVIEW YOUR GAME PLAN YEARLY

Reevaluate and update your career game plan each year, whether or not you have made substantial progress during the year. Update it also whenever there are major changes within the company.

As you proceed, remember that some jobs present opportunities for you to learn and grow while others do not. Nearly all jobs have aspects that are unenjoyable or unrewarding. Sometimes you must weigh the positive elements of a job which are fun or enriching against some negative ones, such as low pay or little chance of advancement.

In summary . . .

It will facilitate the development of your career game

plan to view it as a marketing tool with you as the product. To market a product effectively, you must know it well and must know the potential buyers in the marketplace intimately. This chapter has focused on ways in which you can accomplish that. The remainder of this book provides you with the marketing tools—the political skills—needed to succeed in reaching your goal.

A simple summary of the psychopolitical office primer which follows is that in order to get ahead (or even remain in place!) *you must lead your superior, peers, and subordinates.* You must also learn *when and when not to talk, when and when not to listen, and when and when not to write.*

A skeptic might suggest that these are easy skills and "everyone knows how to use them." This is not true. If you look around you, you will find that most employees operate on a daily basis almost by rote, ordinarily without planning, and usually without any evidence of understanding political skills except by the successful few.

If you learn the political skills and adapt them to your own circumstances, you will suddenly experience an immense satisfaction in knowing that you are doing something positive in controlling your own business destiny!

OUTLINE FOR CREATING A CAREER GAME PLAN

I. Determine the characteristics of your organization.
II. Learn what the organization in general and your boss in particular expect from you in your present position.
III. Analyze your situation by listing:
    A. the things you like doing in the organization;
    B. the things you don't like doing in your work life;
    C. the things you are now doing.
IV. Decide what position you ultimately want to hold.
    A. Compare the lists to determine whether the work you enjoy corresponds to what your boss and the company

expect of you, and whether the company's characteristics generally match the nature of the things you like to do.

B. If they do not correspond, start to develop a plan to find a new and more suitable environment.

C. If they do correspond, select the position in the organization for which you think you are best suited, using the information above.

V. Plan how to get from where you are to where you want to go.

A. Develop a list of stepping-stone jobs from your present job to the one for which you are best suited.

B. Develop a list of the jobs which are to be avoided because they either threaten to lead you away from your goal or to block you from moving ahead.

C. With your lists of jobs to be pursued and avoided in hand, develop a step-by-step map or organizational chart leading from where you are to where you want to go.

D. Determine an approximate time that it will take to move from step to step.

E. List those members of the organization who could help you advance each step along the way.

VI. Review and update your game plan yearly.

Part Two. HOW TO LEAD SUPERIORS

Chapter 4. LOYALTY

I hate ingratitude more in a man
Than lying, vainness, babbling drunkenness,
Or any taint of vice whose strong corruption
Inhabits our frail blood.

—SHAKESPEARE, *Twelfth Night*

Lack of loyalty is synonymous with ingratitude, and Lucifer the Plunger, whose angelic blood might not have been as frail as our own, fell from grace because he thought he was better than his peers and as good as his Superior.

He was once the fair-haired angel, and his name means "lightness" and "the morning star." He was a peer in Heaven with Raphael and Gabriel, but he began to think he was the equal of God. According to the Bible, the morning star fell from Heaven, and Lucifer, the ringleader of the angels who fell, fell first and hardest. This is not to say that Lucifer, whom tradition equates with Satan, did not have his own company of faithless followers.

God knows he did!

God demands loyalty, and the godfathers demand loyalty, and George Steinbrenner demands loyalty, and the bosses of the world demand loyalty. Even the favorite son or the fair-haired boy or the smartest of the angels has a shock coming if he begins to think and talk and act as though he is equal to or better than the individual to whom he owes fidelity and allegiance.

To advance your career, *you must lead your superior,* and one important step in accomplishing this is to be *perceived as loyal to him or her.*

"BIG" LOYALTY

The extreme example of loyalty cited below may be abhorrent to some, but this loyal employee's career advances. . . .

"Big" Nelson, five foot two and slightly bald, had an exaggerated hero worship for his superior, Charles Kilbridal, Chairman of the Board and Chief Executive Officer of Unlimited Affiliates. "Big" had met Charles ten years before while delivering containers of coffee and buttered Danish from his corner confectioner's store. Charles liked his style, prices, and sense of servitude, and hired him as an assistant.

"Big" was now a Senior Vice-President in charge of six affiliates of Unlimited.

One day while "Big" and I were meeting in his office, Charles called him on the phone. "Big" shot out of his chair and stood straight as a ramrod as he talked to him. He never sat down until he had finished his conversation. He was perspiring profusely.

"Why did you talk standing at attention, 'Big'?" I asked. "Charlie couldn't see you."

"He's the Boss," he said simply. "How else should I treat him?"

Who can argue with success? High-minded judgments about "Big's" loyalty pale beside the fact that he held a job he could never have kept on talent alone; that Kilbridal was happy; and that Unlimited Affiliates was doing well. . . .

> There are as many kinds of Bosses,
> As there are different kinds of sauces.
> —ANONYMOUS

An employee can develop loyalty to his boss only when

he learns to understand his superior's personality and motivations. This is true because bosses, and the majority of other folk, are most comfortable around those who understand them. Such understanding helps an employee accept his or her boss as he or she is, because *to understand is to forgive.*

Among the wide variety of bosses who require special attention from a subordinate is one who seems to require more understanding than the rest. The "Good Old Boy Boss"—also sometimes known as the "Birthright Boss"—is particularly unforgiving of the subordinate whose only interest is in performing well on the job.

Princes grow into kings, and the son of the influential or the wealthy or both is given the best in intellectual training, material goods, money, and manners (such as being taught when to duck the check or bribe the headwaiter). After graduation he takes a position in his father's firm or in a company that is beholden to his father or his family. The Birthright Boss learns early the rules of the "Good Old Boy" system: If you're a WASP and an Ivy Leaguer, you'll fit here; if you're from Notre Dame or Georgetown, you'll fit there; if you're from Brandeis or N.Y.U., you'll suit this company. Geographic and nostalgic kinships, too, may propel the colloquialist upward: A Texan drawl, a midwestern twang, or a Georgian "you-all" can mean the difference between success and failure.

With this kind of employer, your Brooklyn stickball stories are more likely to help you into bigger games and bounce your salary higher than your employment history or college transcript could.

Few employers are equally effective in all areas. If you understand your boss's strengths and weaknesses, you'll be far more valuable to him, since you will know the areas in which he is most in need of support. His *modus operandi* is likely to put him in one of two general categories: The Bear Chaser Boss or The Bear Skinner Boss.

THE BEAR CHASER BOSS

These intrepid leaders rouse the bears from hibernation and bestir the bulls, and promote more money and publicity than they need for a still hazy enterprise. They have wildly solid ideas and imagination to match, and catch the fancy of the public and the analysts and the business community. They invent planes or reactors or new revolutionary toys or companies with potential profit-taking tentacles in all corners of the earth.

Usually charismatic, they operate beautifully in high-profile positions which attract a great deal of attention. The satisfaction for this type of manager comes from creating opportunities and generating enthusiasm on a grand scale. His vitality wanes when it's time to turn the opportunity into a serious business venture and make a profit.

Once the Bear Chaser Boss has lured the running bear after him into the tent, he is too bored to proceed with the head-knocking and skinning.

The recent founder of a large department-store chain typifies the Bear Chaser Boss. His ingenuity was responsible for the formation of a billion-dollar company in just a few years. His achievements earned him a cover story in *Time* magazine and the distinction of being named one of the five most important men in the history of retailing by the Harvard Business School.

The company never achieved the level of profits enthusiastically predicted for it, for as soon as it was built, the originator lost interest. He hated the desk work so much that he refused to have either an office or a desk. If anyone wanted to meet with him, it had to be in a coffee shop or someone else's office. Attempts to reach him by phone invariably ended in frustration for the caller. His calls would be transferred from one office or department to another until the caller either hung up in disgust or the company switchboard operator reluctantly took a message for him that, more often than not, never reached him.

Eventually the business was sold to someone who enjoyed the everyday job of running a business—a Bear Skinner.

THE BEAR SKINNER BOSS

Although admittedly not an originator or entrepreneur, this administrator knows what to do once he has the bear inside the tent. He knows how to whomp it, how to skin it, how to package it, how to keep his other skinners happy, how to market the pelts and be apportioned a fair price for his logic and his labors.

This type of boss often has no interest in how the business was created or who started it. He or she is interested only in producing current profits, and is always referring to "the bottom line."

One of this country's largest conglomerates is headed by a Bear Skinner Boss. A few days after his company acquired a controlling interest in a paper-box manufacturing company in Norfolk, Virginia, he visited his new acquisition and called on the company president. After exchanging a few pleasantries, he informed the president that he thought the company's payroll was one third too high. He requested a list of the company's executives and nonchalantly crossed out every third name, oblivious to their positions or duties. He then stood up, handed the list to the president saying "fire them," and left for the airport. The president protested as the door closed in his face, but within the week the eleven fated executives were dismissed. This bear skinner had a bear in his clutches, and he was proceeding to skin it.

A clear-cut understanding of the kind of boss you have enables you to relate to him more effectively, and may prevent your insulting or angering him by inappropriately calling him a "Bear Chaser," for instance, when it is "Bear Skinning" in which he takes real pride.

Whatever kind of boss you have, if he knows you are loyal

and that you support the kind of person he likes to be, you will be allowed to lead him.

Two words of caution seem worth mentioning, however.

WORD ONE: DON'T TRY TO UNDERSTAND EVIL

If you find that your interactions with a superior—or anyone else in your life—are consistently harmful to you, the best policy is avoidance. There are those who are enticing yet from whom everyone seems to walk away injured. Perhaps the attraction lies in flirting with danger. With repeated contact you will begin to understand the motivations of their harmful behavior. To understand everything is to forgive everything, and you might eventually forgive them enough to resume contact and again be harmed by the relationship.

Your best defense in such cases is not allowing yourself to understand them; instead, *harbor your misunderstanding.*

WORD TWO: AVOID BLIND LOYALTY

If your loyalty is so narrowly focused on your superior as to disregard his peers, you may find yourself mired in your job as his sidekick. The peers may see you as a one-man guy or gal and avoid you.

Such blind loyalty may also nurture your superior's possessiveness of you; if he sees you as his personal lackey, he may thwart your progress elsewhere.

Use mature judgment and show loyalty to your superior's peers when appropriate—that is, when you are working with them. In other words, keep your eyes open!

DAY-TO-DAY LOYALTY

The average superior, of course, is not seeking "blind loyalty." He merely wants your undramatic, day-to-day loyalty because in his position he has definite security and parenting needs.

He may feel safe enough to *let you lead him* if you can help him meet his needs:

1. He needs to trust that you will report to him, and only to him. He doesn't want to be undercut with his superiors by his subordinates. He doesn't want anybody on his team going around left flank or behind his back to tell tales to his boss.

2. He wants to feel that he has a strong division or department. In terms of his organizational "family," he wants teamwork and no fighting among the kids!

3. He likes to feel that his "family" is well balanced and healthy without having to call in the "doctor," i.e., consultants.

4. He wants his corporate "children" to obey and respect his fatherly (or motherly) direction, without grumbling or second guessing.

5. When his actions are about to injure his image or endanger his security, *loyalty* means disagreeing—or pulling him in from the brink of professional disaster—in *private counsel.*

6. He will recognize your loyalty in your efforts to instill respect for his actions, ideas, plans, and personality in other company employees.

7. He wants to feel that your loyalty extends to protecting his name among your peers, other employees, and the community, even if an indiscreet action has made him a target for criticism.

8. Loyalty means making efforts *not* to talk about all of the big and little secrets of his life.

Loyalty, as defined above, will nurture your superior's security and parenting needs, and you will lead him.

BRAGGING

When conversing casually with your boss, don't make a big point about the fact that: you drive a more expensive car; you have a lower golf score; you have a higher tolerance for Jack Daniels, Dubonnet, or Chivas Regal; you have fifty-yardline seats for the high school championship game or the

Super Bowl while your boss is stuck in the end zone; you play more expert cribbage or bridge or squash or tennis; your kids are smarter; your speeches are funnier; your roses are bloomier; your humor is wittier; your suits are more stylish; your spouse is more attractive; your deportment is more proper; your hair is thicker and neater; your step is springier; your appetite is fancier; your hobbies are more interesting—cuz, chum, if you brag about it, you'll probably be panned by your boss as a disloyal nonsubordinate.

Disloyalty to a superior can have a significant influence on your business destiny.

WHISTLEBLOWING

Don't be the one to blow the whistle . . .

Woe to the Whistleblowers, for they shall be called traitors throughout the land. They shall be blackballed in every personnel office in the country and lands beyond. It would have been better for them had they bitten off their tongues, not rocked the boat, and wiped up the spilled milk.

A tale of whistleblowing:

"He was really never one of us," a spokesman for his former company proclaims. "Let me tell you about the things that he did wrong. . . ."

But Whistleblower keeps trying:

"Well, Congressman, these are the shameful facts as I have documented them: The Purchasing Department bought seven thousand rivets. Quality Control determined that they were bad, but top company management decided to use them anyway. As a result, five thousand sand buggies broke down just two days after the warranty ran out. And you know our troops are counting on these vehicles. What are you going to do?"

"That allegation is a lie, and the allegator knows it!" cries the company spokesman.

The congressman figures Whistleblower has one vote and

never makes a political contribution; the company is good for a bit of help at election time, and additionally has 399 employees whose jobs might be endangered if the rivet bit got to the press.

"I'll tell you what," the congressman punts. "I'll check into your serious allegation and get back to you."

He calls the company president, and they discuss the accusation of the errant employee over drinks and dinner at the club. Shortly thereafter, Whistleblower gets an innocuous letter from his congressman. And so it goes. . . .

It is considered disloyal to act the offended engineer or financial executive or safety manager who suggests that his shipbuilding company is not blameless when a canoe disintegrates on impact. They could have fixed it with one more coat of glue, but top management decided to save a buck on each item. He calls Jack Anderson, Evans and Novak, Art Buchwald, Ann Landers, and Polly's Pointers. Ann Landers does a column on how to act at a funeral, and Polly writes a how-to column on fixing canoes.

We have all read Sunday feature stories about the individual who has a twenty-four-hour glow of righteousness as he tattles from his soapbox of the sins of his former company.

"Where is Shamus O'Farley today? Shamus O'Farley, who stunned the bubbly world of beer several years ago by reporting that the President of Hops Beer, his employer of twenty-seven years, was skimming the profits from the beer, is living comfortably here in Philadelphia, a stone's throw from the Liberty Bell. He and his wife and family of eight enjoy the true togetherness of their one-room apartment. O'Farley, who has applied for the job of stand-in for the running scenes in the soon-to-be-filmed *Rocky III*, says from his sickbed, 'My conscience is clear.' "

And so are his cupboards.

Such obvious disloyalists seldom find the road home again.

QUESTIONING BASIC POLICIES
OUT LOUD

Even if you merely question the environmental protection standards, or the cost-cutting and life-endangering quality-control practices of your company in internal discussions and memorandums, you could be in big trouble and branded as disloyal. You might not be sentenced to hellfire and Philadelphia like O'Farley, but you will undoubtedly be banished to Limbo and have your ladder of success trimmed at the current step. No longer will you receive memos of importance or be invited to meetings that matter. You will be snubbed and dubbed as "not one of us." Your coffee will no longer be served in the company china but in an economy-size Styrofoam cup.

Most large companies in this country and throughout the world have fostered an aura of nobility among their employees and in the communities they serve, and have knighted themselves in secret ceremonies as oracles of infallibility. It is ironic to question whether or not their benignity is sometimes malignant:

"In a statement issued today from the headquarters of the Build Your Own Nuclear Reactor Corporation, Siegfried Smith, president of the giant corporation, said in part: 'We are a new and growing industry, ready to provide energy for every family in America, if they can ante up the token $2,000 for our product. We care not for profits so long as they have heat and food. We care not for bonuses or yachts. We care only that our children and young second wives are warm and fed.'

"Mr. Smith pooh-poohed the report that several of his top executives had asked him to make the lead walls surrounding the core-manufacturing facility thicker than a quarter of an inch. 'The suggestion was reviewed and rejected,' Mr. Smith said. 'I suggested to those who had submitted the idea that they might be happier working in our uranium mines in the Antarctic, and the fact is they left today on a reclaimed troop train. Their families may or may not be joining them later.' "

Over the years most companies develop an organizational mythology concerning their socially redeeming value and their importance: to the city's economy, to the industry they represent, to the welfare of the consumer, and so on. Loyalty to the organization is a natural extension of the corporate fiction that an organization has some long-range altruistic reason for existence.

Resist the temptation to puncture this delusion publicly, or even privately among intimates. Even if you know your organization to be involved in some wrongdoing (ethically, environmentally, in its dealings with government officials or with foreign governments, etc.), it is unwise to speak out unless the issue represents for you a *true crisis of conscience*, for which you are prepared to take the consequences no matter what. Exposing an important issue that affects top management directly can have serious implications.

You will know if the time has come to speak out, not because the desire to vent your feelings is like an itch that wants to be scratched (don't scratch), but because you feel yourself crossing the line between loyalty as a useful political technique and loyalty that is eroding your essential self-respect.

Be able to play "You Bet Your Job" . . . but rarely.

This brings up again the critical question of the relationship between personal moral beliefs and political skills. That political skills are a means and not an end is illustrated by the *"You Bet Your Job" Theory* (also called the Waldman Theory, after Joel Waldman, its originator).

The *"You Bet Your Job" Theory* states that you needn't risk your career over the continual small skirmishes in any company regarding issues of right and wrong, or appropriate behavior for individuals and the organization as a whole.

In most battles, good political skills will enable you to modify the behavior of a colleague (typically, a superior)—or even of the organization—in the desired direction, either by deterring the Boss from doing something he shouldn't or encouraging him to do something he should, or by discouraging the company from doing something it shouldn't or prompting it to do something it should.

Craftsmanlike political maneuvering will *usually* produce the desired results without undue risk to your own position. Realistically you can expect to win some and lose some. Once in a while you may confront a major issue, a basic ethical conflict, a true crisis of conscience. Then should political maneuvering fail, you cannot stop there. You must go on to "You Bet Your Job," which means that you say to your superior or top management: "You will do this over my organizational dead body."

You are about to do things that are politically unwise and will probably lose your job. But you are prepared to do so because the issue is of such magnitude that the odds of political maneuvering (win some, lose some) will not suffice.

You'll always know when it's time to play "You Bet Your Job." It doesn't happen frequently, unless some hidden quirks in your own personal life are prompting you to seek conflict within your organization. If you find yourself in this position often, consider why it is you want to lose your job.

FAMILY LOYALTY

Even in the case of the righteous and sometimes right Whistleblower, the company without integrity still resembles a family: It sticks together for the common good and denies that the dirty wash being aired by one member belongs to the rest. The rationale is that the bad-rivet cover-up was engineered for the company as a whole and not for the benefit of any one *individual* or small group.

Despite this Sword of Damocles hanging over your head,

you have a better chance of surviving and advancing in your career if you are loyal to your superior. But you cannot practice loyalty in a vacuum. Be aware that your peers will also be loyal in their fashions; if they make the judgment that your brand of loyalty is threatening them, their jobs, or their future, they are apt to cut you off at the pass.

Such was the tale of woe of a management seminar attendee, whose identity will remain inviolate behind the innocuous moniker of "Turk":

Turk: It started out sort of funny. I was editing a weekly newspaper in a suburb of Chicago, picking up some advertising support from the local merchants, and pricking the consciences of some politicians and the top brass at a local plant that turned out widgets for the Army.

Me: What's a widget?

Turk: I want to keep real products and real people out of this. If I tell you and your friends who they are and what they made, you might not want to use or buy or ride in a widget anymore.

Me: That's clear enough. Go ahead, Turk.

Turk: I had blasted the plant in an editorial, and wrote that the Wonder Widget Corporation, which was making the widgets for the military, would move out of town if the government insisted they buy the plant. It was a sort of think-guess piece, but it touched a lot of nerves. They denied my conclusion, but the next week they offered me the job of public relations director at the plant at double the bread I was pulling from the paper.

Me: You kneaded that bread, right, Turk?

Turk: A little later it's not so funny! My first boss was a rough-and-regular, white-haired ex-automobile manufacturer named "Juicy Fruit" Pershing. He was about fifty-five or sixty, and he was a guy with a hardball, right down the middle every time. No curves. No spits. No tricks.

A few weeks later, when he realized I could write a letter

and answer a memo, he called me into his office. He said that if I could successfully handle the tons of questioning memos coming daily from the head honcho at corporate and "get him off my back, I'll kiss you on Main Street." I did the memos, all right. "Juicy Fruit" never did kiss me, but he made me his assistant: assistant to the president. Not bad for a paper boy, right?

Me: So far, Turk, everything is coming up roses. When do we get to the sad part?

Turk: Lydia Lucifer was "Juicy Fruit's" executive secretary, executive assistant, executive coffee maker, prima ballerina, and indispensable Girl Friday. She'd been in the job for ten years and did everything except arouse or dull his lust. She wasn't the type for either, and "Juicy Fruit" never believed in mixing business with pleasure. When my peers heard her royal commands, delivered with cold confidence, they dropped everything, ran, and obeyed.

Me: Apparently, Lydia Lucifer was the fly in your loyalty ointment, right, Turk?

Turk: I was as loyal to "Juicy Fruit" as any employee could be! I didn't just practice or feign loyalty. I believed in him deeply. I worked for this man and respected him. I even had the sense to recognize that my loyalty might seem a threat to my peers, so I helped them polish their images, too, and they were content.

Me: Where did you go wrong?

Turk: One morning in May of my fourth year, "Juicy Fruit" was caught playing show-and-tell with the wife of a podiatrist. The doctor unexpectedly bolted home between patients and noticed his wife had forgotten her pajamas. And there was "Juicy Fruit." The doctor self-righteously spread the word of the rendezvous at Rotary, the diner, among his patients, and up and down the cocktail circuit.

Me: How were you involved?

Turk: When anyone approached me, I'd turn them off and defend the immense humanity of "Juicy Fruit." "Let's forget it, fellows or gals," I'd say. "It could happen to anyone." They were good about it, too.

But not that queen bee in his office! She knew all the lurid details of the incident from the doctor's wife herself because they were phone buddies. She saw a heaven-sent opportunity to put the screws to me, if you'll pardon the expression, because I had been encroaching on her territory. She had the comfortable advantage of being neither a peer nor a superior but squatted majestically on the rung in between.

She watered and fertilized the idea with "Juicy Fruit," who was looking for spies in every shadow, that I was the one spreading the story of the foot doctor's wife in the plant and throughout the community, and was laughing behind his back. He believed her, since he was willing to believe anything to mitigate his own guilt, and told me so in an emotion-packed rage as he read me out of his will and the company. My loyalty program and plans had been torpedoed by a reluctant virgin.

THREE MORALS FROM ONE TALE

There are several morals to Turk's tale. The *first* is that executives often imagine their secretaries to be their mothers and incapable of evil. If your boss is one of those, make sure his secretary thinks she's your mother, too. But then don't make the same mistake with your own secretary!

Secondly, Turk should have known sooner he was in hot seltzer with his boss by reading the queen bee's behavior earlier. He could have gone to "Juicy Fruit" and cut the cutthroat off at the pass.

The fastest way to get an accurate picture of the politics of an organization is to watch the Boss's secretary. You quickly learn who is in and out of favor by how she treats the various players. She is generally reflecting the Boss's view. The Boss may conceal his opinions from everyone else, but when he needs someone to talk to, who else but momma secretary?

Or you? Why shouldn't he be able to talk with you if he knows you're trustworthy and loyal . . . ?

Finally, even if you are not the type of person who is out to "get" someone, someone might be out to "get" you. Don't make the naïve assumption that your noble business ethics are universal!

DON'T CATCH YOUR BOSS WITH HIS PANTS DOWN

Ralph was an administrative assistant to the top boss of Systematic Destructions Enterprises. He and his boss were unusually empathetic, and the latter treated him as if he were a favored son.

Ralph owned a small cottage on the shores of Lake Erie which he offered for a week to his boss, who was embroiled in a messy divorce proceeding brought on by reports of his Casanova-like cavorting. The Boss gratefully accepted the offer, having been assured that his subordinate would stock such necessities as steak and Scotch and corn muffins. He then asked if Ralph would stay with him and his inamorata for the week.

The Boss drove the Cadillac up to the cottage on the selected Sunday. After a flurry of awkward introductions, the week went well enough, but the Boss's true love consistently said things that made her look foolish. The Boss could tell from Ralph's expression what he was really thinking: Why, with all his money, didn't he pick someone who could carry on a conversation?

When they returned to the world of work, they never regained the same close rapport. Ralph had caught the Boss with his drawers in ignoble descent, and was blamed for it. Because he knew his boss's secret, he was somehow disloyal.

If you attend a convention in Las Vegas with your boss, and you have to help him crawl over the floor to his bed after he has crawled over the stage of the topless recital hall and pinched a showgirl on her pompoms, he won't be grateful to you. You have caught him with his guard and pants down, and you have per se been disloyal.

Anyone who thinks he can cultivate an intimate friendship with a superior and trade on it for a favored position is probably making a mistake. If your boss thinks you know too much about him, he will—in his own best interests—find a way for you not to be around.

SOME JOBS JUST MAKE YOU APPEAR DISLOYAL . . .

Even if you are not a conscience-stricken employee who plays "You Bet Your Job" and is thus deemed disloyal; and even if you restrict your disagreements with management to discreet meetings and memorandums, and thus are viewed as just a *little* disloyal, you may still fall into the disloyal category by virtue of your position in the company.

Each job in an organization has some inherent political advantages and disadvantages. Certain jobs carry more suspicion of disloyalty than others—yet they may at the same time offer some excellent political pluses.

High disloyalty-factor jobs include director of personnel or industrial relations; director of advertising; director of computer operations, and company attorney. These positions require behavior that will eventually appear disloyal either to a superior or to top management. For example, employees generally look to the personnel director to represent them against unfavorable decisions made by top management. When the personnel director carries these grievances to top management, however, he or she is considered disloyal.

The director of industrial relations is viewed as disloyal for siding with the union when he or she is unable to secure union agreement with the settlement management wants.

The director of advertising is considered disloyal when questioning whether the firm can back up the claims the sales department wants to make in an ad campaign. He or she is also subject to disapproval from any superior who considers himself an advertising expert and expects the ad director to employ his cherished—though antiquated—ideas. Should the ad director decline to adapt his campaign accordingly, he runs the risk of accusations that he "doesn't listen to proven ideas," and probably that the campaign is a failure in some way or another.

The head of the computer department is suspected of disloyalty when the machine keeps reporting bad news, and the Boss doesn't want to believe it's true.

The company attorney is seen as disloyal because on occasion he or she must report that the adversary of the company in a legal battle may be on the side of right.

When the structure of a job dooms you to failure before you begin, your efforts to make a success of it can create a kind of living hell. If you anticipate the suspicions of disloyalty associated with your job, you can mitigate much of the danger simply by not mounting a white charger and galloping about as a savior.

In summary . . .

The myriad varieties of bosses all have in common the need for loyalty. A subordinate can control, or lead, the relationship between himself and his superior only when he has earned the trust to satisfy that need.

A loyal trust is built by assuring your superior that you report only to him, and that you will protect him from any dangers that arise in the organization.

For corporate survival your loyalty to the organization as a whole must also be evident. Establish by all that you say and do that you will protect the organization from dangers both within and without.

Be alert to seemingly insignificant ways in which you may be unjustly judged to be disloyal, particularly if your job has high "disloyalty exposure."

Chapter 5. GIVING YOUR BOSS THE CREDIT

Ah, take the Cash and let the Credit go,
Nor heed the rumble of a distant drum! . . .

—OMAR KHAYYÁM, *The Rubáiyát*

Khayyám was expert in the use of rope for tents and other things.

"You're the new president and chief operating officer," Chairman Omar tells Elwood in an emotional scene, handing him enough rope to hang himself. "We need fresh ideas," he encourages, not really meaning it. Then he goes over to the corner office to play possum.

Elwood eagerly grasps his new power and before long fantasizes that he is really running things; that he is the new bugler whose *roo-ti-toot-toots* are being followed throughout the camp.

He takes the cash *and* the credit, and the distant drum he hears heralds a new era for the company, with his ideas . . . Elwood's ideas . . . ushering in a new prosperity.

Omar meanwhile has been carefully watching Elwood's performance. Although he doesn't question the financial effectiveness of the president's actions, he does resent the emphasis on new ways and new ideas and new techniques. Omar's name and contributions to the company are never mentioned or even alluded to by Elwood; and Elwood never gives credit to Omar for building the company or for selecting him from many candidates as the new leader.

Omar calls together his board of directors, who have long paid allegiance to him. The board fires Elwood on command.

"But what happened?" Elwood moans. "I thought I was doing a good job."

You were, Elwood. But you were taking all the credit. *You should have given your boss the credit.* If you had done that, you would have been able to continue doing a good job without being fired for it.

Admittedly, giving your boss the credit for something you have personally accomplished probably runs counter to the way you have thought and acted up to now. We are all egotists to a greater or lesser degree, and we are warmed by the personal recognition we receive for getting the only A in French, for winning the championship game with a running hook shot, for making an entertaining speech to Rotary, for putting out a prize-winning report, or for supervising a winning marketing proposal. Applause may be good for the ego, but smug acceptance of applause is not good for the career. *Remember that after conveying your loyalty to your superior, the next strategy for leading him (or her) is to give him the credit.*

FIGHT THE IMPULSE TO FEED YOUR EGO

When some worthy accomplishment is traceable to you, find a way to deflect the accolades which in the normal course of events would come to you, and see that they go instead to your superior, whether he deserves them or not.

"I know it's an award-winning annual report, Muldoon," you could say to a complimentary peer, "and I was the editor and photographer and layout artist. But I carefully checked every detail with the Boss along the way, and he gave me some creative and innovative ideas."

(Some ideas! He wanted to run photos of himself in three places, accompanied by a discursive piece on his search for a new product line!)

Once you've established a pattern of this kind of behavior, the relationship between you and your superior will improve markedly. He will trust you. He will think that you've finally understood him—that you have come to see how really good and infallible he is.

Giving the credit cannot be a sometime thing; it must be continuous. Systematically giving the Boss the credit is the way to persuade him that in you he has a subordinate who understands and appreciates him, and who can be completely trusted.

Give your boss the credit to protect your job and contribute to your advancement.

It is obvious that the white-collar executive's job is in more danger than ever before. While the unionized worker and the tenured professor are well protected, supervisors and executives are given the pink slip of instant poverty in a number of key industries and businesses every day.

When a company is solid and healthy, the white-collar worker is treated with dignity and deference, and for the most part his career shows slow but steady advancement both in responsibilities and wages and fringe benefits. The personnel department goes by the book, coordinating performance reviews of the "team," and it seems at times that the honeymoon will never end.

BOGEY TIME

When the economic crunch comes to a company, however, there is panic, and the numbers game is initiated in the office of the controller: "We have to get the overhead down. All departments have a bogey of fifteen percent."

What's a "bogey"?

In golf it means one more stroke than par for each hole. In industrial or controller usage, however, it is any numerical standard of performance set up as a mark to be attained, as in a contest. For example, how many people do I have to fire to reach my budget "bogey"? (This is a contest?!)

While studying the numbers in their departments, the vice-presidents cast half an eye toward their employees. Their objective is to reach their bogey without affecting their operations substantially. Because the financial layoff objective can't be met by firing all the clerk-typists (who might make only a third as much as the assistant managers), a number of fairly senior people may find themselves on the street.

When the crunch does come, your position will be much safer *if you have led your boss by being loyal and giving him or her the credit.*

ABOUT-FACE

People consistently ask whether this strategy isn't just a bit too obvious. You may think your superior would quickly see through you and brand you as hopelessly obsequious, a toady. This rarely happens. People in general are so insecure that they tend to accept at face value any praise or credit they can find. Besides, if you're really a good performer and your superior is wise enough to have you working for him, *he's entitled to a certain amount of credit for what you accomplish.*

Remember that your superior is as eager and starved for recognition and praise as the next person. You needn't tell him in so many words that he's done a good job; simply allow him to take credit for the good job you've done. This kind of oblique praise is much easier—and less obvious—than the direct compliment.

But, you protest, you and your boss have been wrangling and arm-wrestling for so long that there's no way you can credibly let bygones be bygones and begin giving him or her credit for what you accomplish. Not so. In situations of severe animosity between the Boss and a subordinate, the superior generally accepts this kind of behavioral change by the subordinate as a genuine personality change. He will soon be telling himself with a great deal of satisfaction that at long last you have seen the light. A good deal of research on the subject of ingratiation reveals that people respond more positively to someone whose attitude changes from anger to friendliness than to someone who starts out with a friendly attitude toward them. They seem to be more flattered by winning over the one who has a mind of his own—who isn't the ingratiating type!

Some readers may resist such a change for fear of what their colleagues—peers or subordinates—will think if, after their long history of calling the Boss a no-good so-and-so, they suddenly do an about-face. Perhaps over the years you have nurtured and developed a set of friends and cronies and drinking buddies of whom you are genuinely fond. Together you have grown accustomed to being on the outside looking in, and you gain a certain satisfaction in mutually complaining about the Boss. The role of dissenter and complainer is familiar and comforting to you, and substantial face will be lost with your friends if you suddenly convert and become one of the apostles.

Choose carefully, for your reluctance to give credit to your boss may have tragic consequences during that inevitable overhead reduction when he has a "bogey" to make. If the economics of the company are forcing him to unload one of his three $30,000-a-year men, and you're the only one of the three who hasn't gone out of his way to praise and give him the credit directly or indirectly, guess who gets the ax?

Learning and using political skills (one of which is to *give your boss the credit*) will not only save your job but will advance your career to the limits of your ability and ambition. If you are to have the healthy work life you envision, establishing this kind of relationship with your superior is crucial. Eventually it will enable you to criticize him without hurting yourself, and to change his behavior without becoming his adversary—in other words, it will help you *to lead him.* This gives you a great deal more control over your own fate than would otherwise be possible.

Additionally, you'll find that when good things happen to your superior, he or she will want to include you. If promoted, he'll want to take you with him; if the department is allocated a bonus pool, he'll see that you get a fair share; if his prestige within the organization grows so that he can hire an assistant, he is very likely to choose you.

At first, you'll probably find that avoiding the credit which is your due and passing it along to your boss is emotionally trying, but after a while you'll discover that it has become a new and rewarding habit. Ducking the credit gets easier and easier as you begin to experience how effectively this enables you to lead your boss.

Give your boss the credit so he or she will welcome your recommendations for change in the organization.

Everyone resists change of one sort or another, and bosses are no exception. But you can learn to lead your boss positively toward the changes you recommend.

The entrepreneurial type of manager is perhaps the most resistant to change. The kind of person who successfully starts and builds up an enterprise often cannot let go of the puppet strings when the appropriate time comes. The organization starts to turn sour and decline in his stranglehold. At one time or another during your career, you are likely to encounter this problem firsthand. Should you find yourself working for such a person, remember that you can't make him let go by confronting him directly and telling him to give up the reins and retire to the farm. It won't work, and you probably won't either after that.

Instead of such direct and probably ineffective action, start planting the seeds ahead of time by crediting him with being the pioneer he once truly was. You can speak often of his years of creating invaluable management systems and significant innovations.

"Most successful entrepreneurs can't adapt to change," you tell him, "but you are different."

You give him credit for every new management idea the company has ever used (even if it was adopted without his knowledge, against his wishes, or while he was on vacation). You state publicly whenever possible that all good ideas, past and present, can be credited to the Boss's flexibility and broad vision.

Eventually, if you have given credit effectively enough, he will develop a public commitment to change; he will find himself dedicated to it because his noble image has become linked to the change process. If this friendly persuasion goes on long enough, the Boss may well find himself in the position of sponsoring a change in regimes—and meaning it.

Give your boss the credit to get him to change his own ways of operating.

For example, your superior regularly schedules important meetings at the end of the day—meetings that inevitably drag on and on into the evening, a poor time to accomplish good work. Others' complaints about the late meetings have earned your superior's resentment, but have not changed his behavior. You want to put an end to the late meetings. What do you do?

Instead of criticizing the Boss, you somehow give him credit. You tell him how his hard work and dedication have helped the organization; how his long hours of toil, sacrificing his family life and leisure time, have advanced the interests of the company. You imply that his people respect and admire his unmistakable commitment, his unremitting energy.

After giving him credit in such digestible variations, you

point out that, unfortunately, his subordinates may not be as strong as he is. You suggest that some of his people, even though they also have the company's best interests at heart, may simply be unable to keep up with him; that the quality of their work, the product of the meetings, might well improve if he holds them earlier in the day.

You have succeeded in criticizing your superior's behavior without actually criticizing him. As far as he is concerned, at least one of his subordinates understands and appreciates him; he can now afford to stop calling late meetings to prove how dedicated he is. You have changed his behavior and earned his trust.

There are occasions where you may want to give your boss the credit to change a behavior of his or hers which is unwise politically or is breeding employee discontent. Productivity as well as morale can be seriously affected when no one in a department has the political skills necessary to handle a conflict with the Boss.

While the problem may stem from a boss's refusal to listen to logic, it may be that logic is on his side. In either case, a subordinate has little hope of success with pure reason. His best plan is to develop the sort of practical political skills used by Sam in the true case which follows:

The problem revolved around rumors that the chief of a public works department in a midwestern city was using the department's chauffeured cars to ferry his wife about on shopping trips. Sam, the director of administrative services, was most affected because the chauffeurs were on his staff. The level of resentment in his department had become serious.

Logic, in this case, seemed to be on the side of the chief, whose "abuses" of the departmental cars actually involved his legitimate requests that the chauffeurs drive his wife home alone from official ceremonies they both attended. Drivers' complaints to coworkers fueled their bitterness, however, and morale was dropping. Because the chief felt justified in this use of the cars, colleagues' earlier criticisms of his behavior were ignored.

The employees then sought professional help, and Sam was coached on *how to change his supervisor's behavior by giving him the credit.* Sam met with the chief and told him, "Look, it is unjust for people to criticize you for using the departmental cars to pick up and drop off your wife for occasions like the groundbreaking. She should be paid for accompanying you on city business like that; after all, she has to give up her dinner and her evening, and she isn't compensated. The least she can expect is to be picked up and taken home afterward."

Sam had *given his boss (and his wife) credit* for dedication above and beyond the call of duty. And then he said, "But you must be aware, Chief, that whenever you use the departmental cars for your wife, people are going to criticize you for it, no matter how unjustifiably."

This ploy was not immediately successful, but after Sam's repeated variations on the same theme, the chief one day mentioned casually to Sam that he had decided to stop using the departmental cars for his wife.

OVERCOMING EMOTIONAL BLOCKS

Sometimes when you're working to change a superior's behavior by giving him the credit, you'll encounter an obstacle in the form of a major emotional block on his part. In this sort of situation, solutions based on logic simply cannot work. To counteract an emotional problem, you must design an emotional solution. To insist on using logic under these circumstances can be detrimental to your career.

Joe President assigned his two vice-presidents the job of solving some urgent warehousing problems. This seemed a simple task, except that no one in-house knew much about warehousing, and Joe President distrusted and instantly disliked all consultants. Or so it seemed.

Roy Logic, the R & D (Research and Development) vice-president, was logical in his solid research. He inquired at the local university's school of business, contacted the American Management Association, and spoke to several professional consultants' organizations. He developed a preliminary list of consultant candidates, wrote for and received their credentials, and selected three top people. He submitted their names and qualifications in a logically flawless memorandum to Joe President, including his recommendation on the man to retain for the warehousing problem.

His attitude (and it came through clearly in his memo) was that the only right thing for Joe President to do was to put personal consultant prejudices aside and hire a really good warehousing consultant, preferably the one he recommended.

Joe President never answered Roy Logic's memorandum.

Frank Politico, the financial vice-president, used a different approach. He searched out the backgrounds of some leading consultants in the warehousing field and found one who had gone to the same university as Joe President. They had also been members of the same fraternity. Though not a superstar in his field, Wilson Comisk's credentials were quite respectable and his track record was solid if not inspired. Frank then found a way to mention casually to Joe that a fellow alumnus of his was now a well-known warehousing consultant.

Joe perked up, "Old Wilson the Commy! I wonder who ever married him!"

A few weeks later, having contacted his school chum himself, Joe suggested that they hire him to solve their problems. "Good idea," said Frank.

Roy Logic went back to his office and burned his flawless memorandum.

Shortly thereafter, at a corporate meeting, Frank Politico

gave a progress report on the solution of the problem. "At Joe's suggestion," he began, "we've retained an excellent warehousing and distribution consultant."

The headquarters people were more than satisfied. When his financial vice-president had concluded his presentation, Joe took the podium and said, "I've put Frank in charge of this project and I must say that he's doing a fine job."

Frank Politico had orchestrated a solution that succeeded in overcoming the emotional obstacle represented by Joe's prejudice against consultants. He did this not with logic, but by appealing to a competing emotion in true political fashion. When he maneuvered so that Joe was drawn into making the initial consultant contact himself, Frank knew of and capitalized on Joe's inordinate need to look good to fellow alumni. Nor did Frank neglect the more elementary political aspects of the situation: *He made sure that Joe got the credit* for solving the warehousing problem in front of his superiors at corporate headquarters.

It seems clear enough that Roy Logic's approach could not have succeeded in changing Joe President's behavior, whereas Frank Politico's emotional-political ploy worked. For all his trouble and commitment to the logically right answer, Roy got no thanks whatever. In fact, his relationship with his superior deteriorated significantly during that period, because in order to forestall responding to Roy's well-researched and logical memos, Joe resorted to avoiding him in the office.

The average logical manager who reads this story tends to shudder in disbelief at the idea that Frank advanced his career even though he recommended hiring someone who was not, objectively speaking, the most qualified candidate for the consultancy.

Like it or not, the most logical answer is not always the right answer. From a political perspective, the best solution to a problem is not the "ideal" solution, but the one that ensures peace and quiet in the ranks and still gets the job done. When you've developed the ideal logical solution to a problem but see that it could be politically disastrous, give it up—no matter how attached to it you are. Find an alternative that works and is politically sound. Never let your political judgment be clouded by pride of authorship.

PROMOTE A NERD?

Suppose your boss is a nerd; his management style is disorganized and even chaotic. He is notorious for his habit of getting what he considers a good idea over the weekend, stalking into the office on Monday morning, and telling every executive he meets in the hall on his way to his desk to start work on the idea right away. The idea, born at Saturday's cocktail hour and fermented on Sunday, is now *ipso facto* a project.

The Monday morning bombshell (or stink bomb, as one underling described it) generates a lot of unnecessary and confused activity, with a number of vice-presidents all working energetically at cross-purposes on a project which may not be worth doing in the first place.

What recourse does one have with a boss like that?

The recommendation stands: Even if your superior is incompetent, your best course is still to try to make him look good and to give him the credit.

Why?

It's really not healthy for you, nor good for your career, nor indeed very much fun, to be working for an incompetent. If your superior is really bad, your best course is to work at making him look good until he gets promoted. Getting him promoted is the safest way of being rid of him.

TO TRANSFER OR NOT TO TRANSFER

You could try to get yourself transferred instead, of course, and logically this makes sense; but it is not a good idea politically. Your motives will become evident to your superior in one way or another if they aren't already. To save face, he'll let it be known that you were always something of a troublemaker.

Besides, if you like your job, and if it's only your superior you're dissatisfied with, you shouldn't have to change jobs just to be rid of him. Your ultimate goal, remember, is to take charge of your own life, not to surrender control to your superior—competent or otherwise.

WHY NOT GET HIM FIRED?

But, you may wonder, if he is really incompetent, perhaps you could arrange to get him fired. If you work at making him look bad, at showing him up for the incompetent he really is, wouldn't the appropriate people at corporate soon get the idea and decide to let him go?

Not necessarily. It would depend on how well trained he himself is politically, and on other factors beyond your control. He could have some solid friends in high places.

And suppose you tried to get him fired and didn't succeed? Then *you* clean out *your* desk. Besides, even if you did manage to get him fired, you'd be looked on as the hatchet man and would quickly become persona non grata in your own organization. No other superior would want you around once you'd openly exhibited the most dangerous skill of all: the power to get someone fired.

Still, you say, you'd hate to see an incompetent like your superior get promoted. Couldn't you somehow arrange to get him transferred laterally instead?

Yes, you probably could. But that is the worst possible alternative you could choose. After you were successful in getting him transferred, he'd be continually waiting for a chance to even the score.

The old adage that tells us "Never try to shoot a king and miss" applies equally in organizational life. Moving your superior over—but not out—is as dangerous as if you'd tried to get him fired and failed. For the rest of his career he'd be working as hard as he could to get even. Whoever became your new superior would learn quickly of your lack of loyalty and would treat you like a leper.

The best way to be rid of an incompetent superior, then, is to *give him as much of the credit as possible*, to make him look so good that he gets promoted out of your life.

HOW TO LEAD:

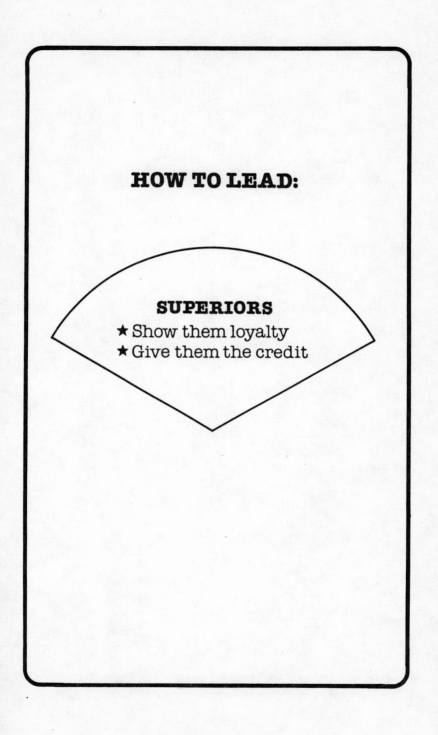

SUPERIORS
★ Show them loyalty
★ Give them the credit

Part Three. HOW TO LEAD
SUBORDINATES

Chapter 6. ORGANIZATIONS ARE LIKE FAMILIES

All happy families resemble one another; every unhappy family is unhappy in its own fashion.
                              —TOLSTOI, *Anna Karenina*

The "happy" families have achieved a desirable balance
with the parents and children living together in mutual
respect. The "unhappy" ones have a diversity of problems,
but commonly suffer from abandonment of authority or
authority ill-handled.

The 1979 World Series Champion Pittsburgh Pirates made
much of the fact that they were a "family," using as a theme
song the disco hit "We Are Family." Their fans in Pittsburgh
and across the country responded to this image of a real family relationship among nonfamily members.

Throughout this section on *How to Lead Subordinates* (an
important wedge in your political action pie), consider that
every organization (a company, division, department, or work
team) is *like* a family:

An organization has *superiors*; a family has *parents*.
An organization has *peers*; a family has *siblings*.
An organization has *subordinates*; a family has *children*.

Logical skills are more important when leading subordinates than when leading superiors or peers, because subordinates require the clear direction of good logical thinking.

But this need for clarity in no way reduces a subordinate's requirement for sensitive understanding of his or her emotional and political needs.

Your subordinates, of whatever age or sex, look to you for leadership. They look up to you and, like it or not, you are a parent figure to them. In your organizational family, you are like a *father* or *mother*; acknowledging this and relating to your subordinates as equitably as you would to your *children* facilitates relationships with them. If you treat them with the concern, interest, and fairness with which you would treat actual children, *you will lead them.* It is not suggested that you go around patting your subordinates on their little tousled heads or promising them trips to the zoo, but the emotions and feelings of subordinates toward their superiors are remarkably parallel to the emotions and feelings of children toward their parents.

To lead your subordinates effectively, you must be—as with children—completely *aware of what they expect* of you as a person; along with this awareness, you must be *responsive* to the wide range and variety of their emotions and feelings. Leading your subordinates is a necessity for your future success.

A prime rule in *treating the children fairly* is to avoid exclusive socializing with any one subordinate, male or female —not even one of the guys or gals who could make an interesting drinking buddy, since you both talk the same language. It demoralizes and demotivates the rest of your subordinates.

Meet with subordinates both individually and as a group, regularly . . .

When our children were small, we, like many other families, instituted a "family meeting." Because of the press of everyone's schedules and responsibilities, the weekly event took place following Sunday afternoon dinner. As the father, and therefore the biggest and smartest (a fact often quietly questioned by the other members of the meeting), I invariably assumed the role of chairman and called the assembly to order by tapping my dessert spoon against my empty wineglass. I then called the roll, which was more of a formality than a necessity, since you can't go too many places on a Sunday afternoon when you're eight, six, or four years old. Each family member was asked in turn to voice any observations, suggestions, or criticisms that may have been bottled up during the preceding week. The first meetings produced little of merit except my confirming with my wife the opinion that we had cute and smart offspring.

Before long, the children, no longer confused by my condensed version of *Robert's Rules of Order* and encouraged by their own growing parliamentary experience, contributed to various improvements in our family life. Concrete results of their suggestions and criticisms included the moving of Sunday dinner from 4 to 6 P.M.; the banning of hair curlers from the dinner table; the replacement of Jamie's ballet lessons by ballroom dancing; and the imposition of a curfew on noisy adult exuberance after 10:30 P.M., except on New Year's Eve and every seventh Saturday.

These family meetings proved an excellent way of building family unity. They formalized a method of conveying to our children our desire to understand their problems and frustrations and triumphs, and of giving them the help and counsel they wanted and needed.

As a family meeting contributes to unity and understanding between parents and children, a similar meeting between you and your subordinates can be a vital ingredient of successful leadership. Call your subordinates together on a regular basis. Originate an agenda for each meeting and encourage everyone to add items of interest. Avoid a mood of stiffness because it inhibits subordinate participation, thereby restricting the effectiveness of the meeting as a means of unifying your group. As chairman, encourage everyone to express his or her opinions, convictions, criticisms, humorous observations, or clichés. This inspires increasing closeness among the subordinates in your organizational family.

HOW TO PLAY "TOUCH-THE-BOSS"

Another technique to promote unity is to play "Touch-the-Boss." Children need to touch their parents in a friendly way. The correlation is that the subordinates want to touch the Boss. Since you want to promote productivity during the day, small talk has no place. But subordinates need some form of friendly interaction with you. This need can be met by starting an informal ritual—perhaps once a month—of inviting your staff to have a casual chat with you for an hour or so at the end of the day.

Choose an atmosphere comfortable for all of you. If your office is such a place and light alcoholic beverages are allowed, then use it. Otherwise find an outside meeting room. Keep the talk light: no business, if possible, and definitely no decisions!

By recognizing your subordinates as individuals and at the same time prompting them to meet with you and each other as a cooperating unit, you will be building your group into a team. Happy teams with all the pieces together are melded into an organization in a way not possible for diverse individuals. Headed by a strong leader or leadership group, such teams are effective working units.

Don't neglect ordinary everyday amenities . . .

It's easy to fall into the habit of taking for granted those close to us whom we see regularly. A simple hello or good-bye is an important acknowledgment to those who work for us.

In each closing sequence of the TV series *The Waltons*, everyone says good-night to everyone else as the lights click off one by one. Various versions of this ritual are probably repeated each night in millions of homes all over the world.

In *The Black Cottage*, Robert Frost wrote, "As a child misses the unsaid Good-night, and falls asleep with heartache. . . ."

As a child needs the reassurance of his parents' love at day's end to ward off dreams of dragons, so your subordinates need a reassuring "good morning" and "good-night" from you.

All children are not the same . . .

As a rose is not the same as other roses, subordinates are not all the same. They don't want a Mr. Nice Guy, but they do want individual treatment. As a parent, you would not treat the child who is three in the same way as you would the one who is thirteen. They would have different standards for bedtimes, for instance, based on their different needs.

Likewise, the subordinate who has been in his job for fifteen years with neither the ambition nor the ability to rise higher bears little resemblance to the new college graduates of both sexes and all races who have recently joined the work force. Their needs and interests are vastly different. Retirement benefits are of primary interest to some, while the intracompany touch-football competition has the greatest appeal to others.

To lead effectively, treat your subordinates as individuals . . . and not necessarily the same . . .

Opinion researcher Daniel Yankelovich has discovered some fundamental changes emerging in the work force which support this recommendation. His polls reveal a decline in the percentage of workers in the United States who are still motivated by traditional monetary and retirement incentives. These workers are most comfortable with strict work guidelines and clear tasks. They do not expect to find "meaning" in their work.

By contrast, an increasingly substantial percentage of the work force reflects a new set of values. Eager for responsibility and more vital work, these employees are seeking a commitment worthy of their talents and skills. Yankelovich concludes, "In the mix of rewards for work, money no longer has the motivating power it once did."

As a superior, you may have to deal with both kinds of subordinates simultaneously and in a manner appropriate to their personalities, needs, and ambitions. Yet each subordinate must feel that his treatment is equal to that of his peers.

For example, you may reward the more traditional employee with a company car or first-class flying privileges. Those holding different values may prefer a tuition-aid program or time off to work for a particular cause or political candidate that sparks their interest.

Good leaders have integrity . . .

Integrity is defined as "moral soundness, honesty, and freedom from corrupting influence or practice." The discovery of a lack of *integrity* in a superior or a parent figure has a very direct and destructive effect on the subordinate or child. The following story, based on fact, exposes a lack of integrity in *both* a family and a company.

A division of the Conglomerate Company with a seven-million-dollar budget decided to change advertising agencies. Caesar, the advertising director, lined up five agencies to make presentations to the executive vice-president and himself. Two of the five presentations came to the top, and the advertising director informed his contacts at each agency "off the record" that they were "in the running."

The Clinton agency, one of the top two, decided to enhance its presentation. Secretly it informed the Conglomerate advertising director that it was prepared to pay $50,000 for the contract, "up front." The director found it impossible to be insulted by such a sum. It novocained his conscience.

The next morning he arranged an emergency meeting with his executive vice-president. To his credit (which is the last he deserved), he was open and honest with him.

They looked at each other and smiled. Who would they be hurting? they rationalized. Clinton *did* have an excellent presentation. "Take it," the VP told the advertising director.

The pickup was set for the Philadelphia airport, where the ad director was to present the official letter awarding the advertising agency contract to the Clinton firm. The ad director, to avoid boredom on the two-hour drive and to give his young son a change from his homework, took along eleven-year-old Caesar, Jr. The father was too nervous for small talk during the drive. He realized his superior hadn't mentioned how they were to divide the money. He reasoned that the VP must intend it to be an even split, or why would he have asked him to be the bagman?

They reached the airport, parked, and proceeded to the airlines booth. Sure enough, there was Caesar's contact with the Clinton agency, armed with a tan attaché case. They shook hands and exchanged their promises.

The father pulled the son into the nearest men's room, relieved that it was deserted. He quickly opened the attaché case. A pile of twenty-dollar bills, nicely stacked, smiled back at him. His son looked at the array and whistled.

"What did you get that for, Dad?" he asked.

Caesar didn't answer. He put his forefinger to his lips, seeking silence. They returned to the car and began the trip home. Caesar's son was bothered. The trip. The money. The silence. His father shouldn't be acting this way. At least, he should tell him what it was all about.

Halfway back, Caesar answered. "He was from the advertising agency we just hired, son," he explained awkwardly. "He owed me some money."

His son was silent the rest of the way.

The advertising director and his son arrived home, and Caesar's wife greeted them coldly. "The executive VP called," she reported. "He wants to know how you made out. Please call him. There are cold cuts for dinner." That figured.

She turned to Caesar, Jr. "What did you and Daddy do?" she asked.

"Daddy picked up a lot of money," Caesar, Jr., said, not quite naïvely.

Caesar called his vice-president and reported the success of his expedition.

The son was increasingly bothered by the airline terminal transaction. His mother, at odds with Caesar for months over sex and other declining joys, tried to answer his questions; she concluded that something "smelled."

"I think your father was paid off by that advertising agency for the new contract he's been talking about," she said.

So the son was now more upset than ever, with his mother confirming his suspicions. His father was bribed? That's wrong!

The wife, who wasn't given any of the "lot of money," continued to play bridge with the company wives, dropping broad hints between her three no-trumps about her husband's probable new prosperity. More in confusion than in joy, Caesar, Jr., spread the word among his friends that his father had mysteriously come into a lot of money. He did not tell them proudly.

This particular case soon came to its unhappy conclusion. Within weeks, the entire transaction had become common knowledge in their circle of acquaintances and quickly reached back into the company, where everyone soon knew of a major payoff made by the advertising firm. Eventually the executive vice-president and Caesar were removed from their positions; the major reason was the bribe.

POOR LEADERSHIP AFFECTS SUBORDINATES AND CHILDREN ALIKE . . .

A most interesting aspect of this incident was that both the real son, who had gone to the bribe-taking with his father, and the corporate "children," the subordinates reporting to Caesar, were equally upset by his behavior. My conversations with Caesar's wife revealed many things their youngster had said about his feelings and his father, such as: "Dad didn't have to do that kind of thing; he made enough money!" "What will I tell my friends if they ever find out all of the truth?" "What will happen to me if he is fired for what he did?"

Caesar's subordinates within the company voiced *the same words, the same questions.* They were angry with Caesar. They said, "With his salary, he sure didn't have to do that kind of thing." They didn't want to work for him anymore, even if he survived. They were deeply ashamed. They showed insecurity (and kinship with the feelings of his son) by asking what would happen to them if Caesar were fired for bagging the bribe. They were angry at him in the same way as his son for exposing them to an unknown. They were angry that he had exposed them without their knowledge or control.

Despite individual differences, children are alike in wanting parents they can respect; despite other differences, subordinates want their superiors to be individuals of great integrity. Both want to be proud of those directing their personal or business lives.

This true story vividly illustrates the parallels between a parent figure and the head of an organization or department. The corollary is that the behavior patterns which apply to families apply to the business sector as well. The similar reactions of both "families," the real and the organizational one, in the payoff case mark the predictable seismographic effects on children and subordinates when there is a lack of integrity at the top.

Just as "the sins of the fathers" have adversely influenced the future and character of many families (although admittedly the sins of some great-great-grandfathers of the Robber Baron era have been assuaged somewhat by the affluence of their current heirs), so the chicanery, bribery, and dishonesty of top company officials will eventually filter down to their "children," the subordinates, with wrenching emotional and financial consequences. The leadership of the company is to blame. Most subordinates follow their leaders and are themselves corrupted to the detriment of the entire organization.

But the superior is not actually the parent . . .

Although the superior is a parent figure to his or her subordinates, and many rules that apply to gaining leadership in business mirror those that are needed to lead a family well, the superior must never cross the line and *become their parent* in his mind.

Some organization leaders think they *are* parents—that they are and should be the prime element in the lives of their employees. The resulting overdependency stifles the individuality and growth of the subordinates.

Perhaps the origins of this thinking can be traced to the days when the mining company or lumber company or packing company was the only game in town. Anybody who wanted to work for a living had to work there. And after a period of poor pay and high prices, many workers began to "owe their souls to the company store" for requiring such necessities as food, fuel, dresses for the wife, shoes for the children, and a bottle of rye for father.

In companies like the above, you will find the superior who plays Big Daddy to his employees (especially the executive recruits with "potential") and usually makes deals with the "new bloods" long before graduation. The starting pay is better than most, the fringes are great (pension, medical care, vacations), and the persuasive multiscreen indoctrination on "*the* only place to work" takes about two weeks, with evenings off for good behavior.

You can spot these caricatures of paternalism by their solicitous interest in your spouse or intended:

"Does he or she play bridge, golf, racketball, Ping-Pong?

Is she into crewel, watercolors, needlepoint? Can he hold his martinis? Is she now or has she ever thought of being pregnant? Does he do volunteer work? What kind? (Try to have him stay out of the inner city!) Can she cook? Does he snore?"

Everyone dresses alike except for the Boss, who can wear what he wants. He's Big Daddy, and the employees are part of his family now.

This executive's directives are another giveaway:

"Do community and neighborhood work," (but to a limited degree). "Don't join the Chamber of Commerce or coach Little League or run for local political office." (If you're any good at your job, the company will soon promote you up the ladder and move you far away, like to Cleveland. If you're as good as we think, the Chamber and Little League and the politicos would be mad if we moved you. If you're really not that good, we don't want you representing us there in the first place.)

The worst effect of such overdependency is that it undermines internal motivation and growth. Subordinates who are expected to rely on a superior for their development begin to lose the ability to achieve it for themselves.

In summary . . .

While subordinates are *not children or childish*, they do react in a *childlike* manner to their superiors or leaders.

EQUALITY IN REWARDS

The Child: Each wishes to be treated equal to or better than other children in the family. Example: A client of mine sent back an $11,000 gift from her father because her brother had received $20,000.

The Subordinate: Each wants to make as much or more money than his or her peers. This need for equality includes size of office, secretarial assistance, equipment, and furniture. Example: A company hired inexperienced people at $25,000 a year to expand the department. Longtime and experienced employees were being paid $23,000. When they found out—and they always do—they became extremely upset and began talking about a mass walkout as a protest.

EQUALITY IN TIME

The Child: Each wants equal parental time of good quality. Example: "Dad takes Sue to racketball every Saturday, but he never takes me to a baseball game." Or "If we're together, his mind is on something else or there are loads of people around."

The Subordinate: Each wants equal parts of his superior's time and resents being shut out or ignored. Example: "He never has time to meet with me without the phones ringing and people going in and out. When Joe goes in, he shuts the door and has his secretary hold all calls."

EQUALITY IN IMPORTANCE

The Child: Each wants to be unique and of importance to the parents. He or she is disturbed and resentful when this does not happen. Example: "Everyone says my sister is Dad's favorite, not me." A positive example: "I always look forward to my birthday; my dad takes me to one of the finest restaurants in Georgetown. It's really a special treat!"

The Subordinate: Each wants to be indispensable and wants his or her talents recognized. Example: "She doesn't appreciate what I can do; she treats me as though anyone could do the job." A positive example: "She told me again today that whenever she has a really tough nut to crack, she calls on me."

DESIRE FOR HARMONY

The Child: "Why can't my mother and father get along?

They're always fighting. Why don't they think of us kids for a change?"

The Subordinate: "Why can't my boss and his peers get along? They're always fighting. At the rate they're going, one of them might get canned. Why don't they think of us workers for a change?"

DESIRE FOR THE TRUTH

The Child: Each wants to be told the truth and not kept in the dark about happenings which are important to him or her. Example: "I know Mother's been to the doctor, and both my parents have long faces. Why don't they trust me and tell me what's going on?"

The Subordinate: Each wants to be told the truth and to know the realities of his situation. Example: "I know that the Boss has been to staff meetings every morning this week, and the grapevine says there's going to be a layoff soon. Why doesn't she trust me and tell me what's going on?"

Although a family and an organization are not the same, the rules of good parenting frequently apply to good leadership. Parents and superiors are models whom their children and subordinates emulate. If a parent figure or leader desires harmony and integrity in the family, he or she must exhibit and promote it.

Chapter 7. BE A GOOD ROLE MODEL

Example is the school of mankind, and they will learn at no other.

> —EDMUND BURKE,
> *Letter I, On a Regicide Peace*

With the exception of the instinct of self-preservation, the propensity for emulation is probably the strongest and most alert and persistent of the economic motives proper.

> —THORSTEIN VEBLEN,
> *The Theory of the Leisure Class*

If bribery and gift-giving are the order of the day in a company, employees will *emulate* the accepted style. Even when they are on the receiving end of the corruptive practice, they learn to operate in an unscrupulous business manner.

You, as a superior, will be *imitated*, just as you, as a parent, will be *imitated*. Only gross credulity would lead anyone to expect his or her subordinates (or children) to follow the implicit dictum to "Do as I say; not as I do."

The executive vice-president in the previous chapter who instructed his advertising director to "get the money" from the ad agency forfeited his integrity as well as his job.

Excellent leaders who realize that they are role models,

and that integrity is intrinsic to their being good role models, operate accordingly.

DO AS I DO

Several years ago the new general manager of a California-based division of a Fortune 500 conglomerate became concerned by persistent rumors about "irregularities" in his purchasing department.

Business acquaintances anxious for his favor as headman of the biggest defense industry in the area cornered him at Lions Club luncheons and confided to him—after the chicken and peas and before the dessert—that his purchasing people were reputedly the most corrupt in the state and that this reputation was well deserved.

The general manager summoned the senior members of the purchasing department to the company's main conference room at 2:30 P.M. on a Friday, allowing them time to return from free lunches. His message to the assembled group was short, direct, and vulgar:

"Ladies and gentlemen, and I call you that advisedly. [A few muffled titters.] I have been hearing wild stories of all the bribes and kickbacks and payoffs some of you have been accepting and soliciting from our subcontractors. I can prove it if I have to. It stops right now, or you're out the door. When a subcontractor or a potential subcontractor approaches you with an offer of loot, make sure you can eat it, drink it, or lay it in one day—or don't accept it. Understood? The meeting is over."

All significant corruption and dishonesty ceased. His strong leadership averted the dismissals his staff would have eventually incurred otherwise.

This example is unique because the general manager's speech appears to condone the acceptance of some favors. But on a deeper level, the speech reflects this manager's maturity and realism. He did not try to set a standard by which he himself could not live or enforce. He knew that he would occasionally accept a social lunch from a potential vendor, and that he could not prevent his subordinates from socializing.

He firmly established fair and clear ground rules: Any favors had to be so minor as not to affect the purchasing decisions of the employees. Fully aware of his position as a role model, he was not guilty of saying, "Do as I say; not as I do."

Although his methods may have lacked the polish of a typical Ivy League M.B.A., he had displayed the integrity and courage in his own business practices to back up his demands. If he had been guilty of the same offenses, his efforts to clean up the department would not have succeeded.

If you smoke excessively or drink heavily, spice your language with profanities, and deceive your children or lie in their presence, then you can expect them to regard such mores as acceptable. You'll have little success telling them to eat their dinner because it's good for them if you hide your untouched spinach under your napkin.

You cannot be consistently late arriving at the office, show up twenty minutes after the regularly scheduled start of meetings and then condemn your subordinates for their lack of punctuality; you cannot give or accept gifts in your business dealings and berate or punish your subordinates for doing the same; you cannot lie to your subordinates and expect them to tell the truth; and you cannot shirk your job and your responsibilities and expect those reporting to you to perform to their capacity and potential.

Charles Caleb Colton's famous statement that "imitation is the sincerest flattery" isn't *necessarily* so. Imitation is sometimes practiced by those who find in the actions of their superiors or parents justification for their own behaviors.

You are not treating your children or your subordinates fairly by setting an example inappropriate to a good parent or a strong leader!

If your superiors take the wrong road . . .

As a leader in either upper or middle management, you may at some time be placed in a position which you and your subordinates consider unfair, in conflict with your interests, or endangering to the welfare of the community.

As an example, Company D has been secretly dumping its toxic chemical waste in the town's rivers and streams for years. When this cost-cutting crime is uncovered by an investigator with the Environmental Protection Agency, the executives bluster their indignation and state that they will move out of the area if they "are further persecuted by lackeys of the state and federal governments."

You would appear to be in a lose/lose situation: Your precarious position is that top management expects all its executive personnel to support its stand, while your subordinates seek your leadership against the bad decisions and declarations of the boys on Mahogany Row.

You cannot in good conscience loudly applaud the actions of your superiors. Nor should you, unless you are independently wealthy, trot headlong into the executive offices on a white horse and attack their windmills and windfalls. You *can* tell your subordinates that you agree with them, and that you'll try to convince your superiors it would be in the best interests of Company D and the community if they backed off from the dangerous dumping practices.

Try to work your magic in the communications channels that are open to you without positioning your head directly in the path of the guillotine. When the upper echelon feels many pressures besides your own, it may change its stance, and a crisis will have been averted. *Your group will rightly feel they have been treated fairly by your leadership and support of their opinions.*

If in an extreme case you have to *"Bet Your Job"* and push harder against a management decision than it expects or appreciates, try to spot a nearby tree to which you can comfortably jump. It should be of at least the same height as the one you are leaving. *If this happens, the subordinates you are leaving will also feel they have been treated fairly.*

Do not lie to or deceive your kids or subordinates . . .

Some parents and superiors unhesitatingly lie or deceive their children or subordinates to achieve short-range results. They rarely anticipate the long-range consequences, which may be more harmful to the family or organization than the short-term gains are valuable. Employees, as well as children, recognize lies or deception and invariably find a way to even the score.

The most popular way to justify the deception is to get into an "ends justify the means" syndrome. Management says, "We know the employees will be irresponsible if we tell them the truth, so we are justified in lying to them."

A typical scene concerns the departmental cutback which comes to almost every organization at one time or another. When senior management decides to cut personnel, it may also decide to conceal that information for fear the marked employees will, at best, stop working, and, at worst, respond with theft and sabotage. The scenario ends dramatically as employees are told *on* D-day to clean out their desks and depart.

Top management fails to recognize that it is the biggest loser in this course of action. The remaining employees lose confidence in management's reliability. Fear abounds, because they never know who's next! If told the truth and treated fairly on the issue of severance, dismissed employees usually act responsibly, complete their work, and leave without retribution. But the reverse is often true if the matter has been handled with deception. Such observations support the view of Cardinal Thomas Wolsey that, "Corruption wins not more than honesty."

If your business actions are consistently ethical, you will win the respect and emulation of your subordinates. As they grow confident of your fair and honest treatment of them, *you will lead them!*

MOTIVATE SUBORDINATES TO USE THEIR TALENTS AND SATISFY THEIR WANTS

The focus of the previous chapter, "Organizations Are Like Families," was on the similarities between subordinates and children in their desire for harmony, truth, opportunity, equality of rewards and time, and recognition of individual importance. A superior can help his subordinates satisfy these wants if he motivates them properly.

A *motive* is any idea, need, emotion, or organic state *within* an individual that prompts him to action. How can you motivate your subordinates? What prompts them to action?

*A good job description is an undervalued
motivating tool . . .*

In general, employees want challenging jobs in which they receive recognition for proficiency. *They want a sense of achievement while enjoying their work.*

Job descriptions, much in vogue in some large companies, offer a good way to start motivating your subordinates. Although often dull and unimaginative, a good, up-to-date job description spells out the duties and responsibilities of the position and guides the jobholder's actions.

If your company has job descriptions for your subordinates, obtain copies and review them for completeness, logic, and obsolescence. Once in line with the job as it actually is or should be, the job description can be used to discuss with each subordinate exactly what is expected of him or her.

This revision of the job description can be as important a learning experience to you as it is to the subordinate. While redefining the somewhat valueless standard job description, you will better understand the job you are supervising.

Armed with knowledge of all the duties being performed by your subordinates, you'll be better able to evaluate their performance. You can, therefore, expect better results.

In summary . . .
In Chapter 7 we learned that:
* Having integrity is intrinsic to being a good role model;
* When a good role model relates to children or subordinates fairly, they permit him or her to lead them;
* Such a leader can help subordinates achieve their professional goals.

Just as a child does not want a spineless or an iniquitous parent, a subordinate does not want a corrupt or thoughtless leader to emulate:

* Children and subordinates look to their parents or leaders to fight for their rights;
* Children and subordinates want to live with truth and reality, not with dishonesty, deceit, or desertion;
* Children and subordinates look to a parent figure for recognition and leadership;
* Superiors establish the standard by which their subordinates relate to them as they interact with *their* superiors.

If as a superior you exhibit careless work habits or dishonesty, your subordinates, emulating this behavior, will fail in their jobs. If instead—*as a positive role model*—you articulate your expectations to your subordinates, commending their efforts and achievements, they will strive ceaselessly in your behalf. Your subordinates will do unto you as they see you do unto your superiors. Your professional behavior sets the work habits and ethical standards for those who report to you.

You will be able to deal more fairly with your subordinates if you know and understand their jobs. Helping them develop good job descriptions can give you that knowledge. Establishing goal setting and performance reviews will further ensure that you *treat them fairly,* and will extract from them the maximum of their talent, their learning, and their talent for learning. You will stretch their capabilities to the fullest, and they will be grateful for your leadership.

Chapter 8. THE LAW OF RELATIVITY

The good parent (superior) is *not* concerned with the treatment of his or her children (subordinates) relative to *those of the neighbors* (competitors), but relative to each other.

To wit:

The Albatross Sailing Company up the road gives each of their employees a turkey at Thanksgiving and a goose at Christmas. Your company sends book matches with the company's logotype, wishing everyone a Happy New Year. Your subordinates briefly envy the turkey, look askance at the goose, and laugh a little at the matches. But none of them is angry with you or the company; they are being *treated equally among themselves.*

Of course, if wages and benefits in a similar industry in the same town are double what your company provides, you have a problem. For the most part, however, your subordinates are comparing their salaries, their fringes, their recognition, and their opportunities with each other, and not with the employees of another company.

Managing subordinates equitably and impartially—and thereby motivating and leading them—requires careful evaluation of the processes of:

Goal setting;
Performance review and rating; and
Remuneration.

When viewed against the backdrop of the organization as it resembles a family, these processes move from the purely technical realm to the political. This chapter analyzes each of these disciplines from the functional as well as the political perspective.

Goals are not dreams . . .

To be more than a dream, *a goal must be both measurable and attainable.* For goals to be of value, they must be set by those who are to attain them. But as a superior, you bear the ultimate responsibility for determining whether your subordinates' goals are dreams that will become nightmares or realistic plans for progress which may well come true.

In goal setting with your subordinates, the following procedure is recommended:

1. Ask each subordinate to list:

   a. What he is presently doing;
   b. What he thinks he should be doing;
   c. What he would like to do; and
   d. What he doesn't like to do.

2. Talk over and reach a consensus with each subordinate as to his or her exact responsibilities.

3. Ask each subordinate to set *measurable* and *attainable* goals for all the functions of the position.

4. Ask your subordinate to compare past achievements with the proposed goals, and have him or her clarify how the future might surpass the past.

5. Obtain from each subordinate a plan to attain his or her committed *productivity.*

6. Set a mutually acceptable interim time schedule with each subordinate for all his or her programs or goals so that neither of you has to wait until the end of the year to check progress.

Ideally, the time schedule will call for monthly benchmark meetings that coincide with and become part of your performance review program.

If you are required to use a goal-setting program in your organization that conflicts with these recommendations, do not totally dismiss the one described above. You may be able to adapt your company's procedures along these lines gradually.

Goals are for everyone . . .

The importance of establishing goal-setting procedures for everyone in your group cannot be overemphasized. The temptation is to concentrate attention on the high-visibility employees, whose functions seem more important, and to overlook the lower subordinates. Resist this temptation! Each member of your team affects the morale of the entire group.

The correct utilization of goal-setting principles and procedures will positively affect the morale of your subordinates, both individually and collectively.

You have the final word . . .

As a superior, you are in a position to gain an overview that your subordinates do not have. It is up to you, therefore, to balance the goals and performances of the members, of your team to make the products or perform the services for which your team is responsible.

MEASURING PERFORMANCE

Good performance can be measured by three "Balloons of Performance":

1. VOLUME refers to the number of products, or the dollar amount produced or sold, or the number of functions or services performed.

2. EXPENSE refers to the amount for which products or services are sold as well as the cost to produce, purchase, or perform them.

3. CUSTOMER SATISFACTION refers to the degree to which the products and/or services are meeting the needs and desires of the customers both within and without the organization.

Give everyone three balloons . . .

Whenever possible, each member of your group should have goals that contain all three elements. Obviously some jobs are so narrow in scope that the subordinate who performs them cannot have goals for all three. But the sum total of your subordinates' goals should involve a balance of these three balloons. Their goals are thereby incorporated into your goals.

Imagine, for the moment, that you are the manager of a sales department. The goals of a salesperson in your department might read something like this:

1. I will sell $125,000 worth of books in the year:

$5,000 in January,
$4,000 in February,
$20,000 in December, and so on.

2. My customers will feel that I was attentive yet not pushy.

Your goals as sales manager might include:

1. This department will sell $1,000,000 worth of books in the year:

$40,000 in January,
$30,000 in February, and so on.

2. The department expenses will be $900,000, consisting of:

Cost of books, $500,000,
Salaries, $150,000, etc.

3. Our customers will feel that we served their needs efficiently and courteously.

You will note that your subordinate, the salesperson, did not have an expense goal, although you, the superior, did. In your broader role as manager, you are expected to control expenses. In this way you can balance your goals with those of your subordinates to realize a profit while keeping the customers satisfied.

And keep them all flying . . .

Keeping these three "Balloons of Performance" in delicate balance is the task of the manager concerned with organizational health and high morale. These elements are heavily interdependent on each other. You can't have increased volume—a return of money, or such money-making intangibles as increased productivity—without a planned increase in expenses, or you'll probably puncture the balloon of customer satisfaction. You cannot put the balloons aloft on an individual basis and expect to attain your goal.

If a balloon falls . . .

The Scotch Brands Discount Stores, with a chain of outlets in such prime locations as the Death Valley Mall and the Bermuda Triangle, decide to cut expenses by reducing the number of check-out cashiers. Management does not anticipate the ensuing volume drop, which more than offsets the money saved on salaries. In cutting the number of check-out personnel they overlook the possibility that customers who become disgusted waiting in long and slow-moving lines will walk out without their purchases.

One profit-taking sideline of the salary-saving exercise—shoplifting—increases dramatically. Shoplifters don't have to wait in line.

To the rescue . . .

Sally Sale, a Scotch Brands store manager *par excellence,* rushes to the rescue. When Sally receives word from the home office that she should reduce the number of cashiers in order to cut expenses (Expense Balloon), she anticipates a Volume Balloon drop and decides to change her goals. She then prepares a set of new goals for her superior, reflecting the reduction in cashiers and requesting a small budget increase to retrain stockkeeping personnel to do cashiering. As a result, the head cashier will be able to call on the stock personnel when lines begin to back up.

Sally balances her goals. She knows that the Volume Balloon and Customer Satisfaction Balloon will be adversely affected by tampering with the Expense Balloon.

Her boss approves her request, and Sally works with her subordinate in charge of stock personnel to amend his goals to include the timely retraining of his personnel.

Sally's store is the only one in the Scotch Brands chain which does not suffer a volume drop.

Another balloon down . . .

On another occasion—again neglecting the necessary balance between the "Balloons of Performance"—the Scotch Brands management decides to mark up all merchandise by 10 percent, figuring no one will notice.

Armed with ads, personal budgets, and hand-held computers, today's shoppers notice: Sales drop off, proving once again the old adage that *increasing the price of anything decreases the number of units sold.*

As Sally says, "People aren't as stupid as they look."

But some managers are!

And once again . . .

Sally is undaunted. When she receives the order to raise prices by 10 percent, she realizes that her sales Volume Balloon will probably drop.

This time her request to the home office is for a 10 percent reduction in inventory. She plans to lower her Expense Balloon to balance the anticipated drop of the Volume Balloon. In other words, with higher prices she expects fewer

sales; with fewer sales she needs less inventory. Sally works
with her subordinates, the buyers, to reduce inventory.

As a result of her effective balancing of the "Balloons of
Performance," Sally's profitability is the highest in the chain
that quarter.

Evaluate goals politically . . .

Sally's examples illustrate the political nature of goal setting. If Sally had resisted management's orders to cut cashiers
in the first case or to raise prices in the second, they would
have viewed her as an obstructionist. By readjusting her
goals to continue balancing the various elements of performance, she was able to continue satisfying her realistic
goals.

For your goals to be properly implemented, you need the
commitment of your subordinates to your goals. Constant
interaction with them—to reevaluate those goals, particularly
in the face of changing circumstances—develops that commitment.

Review goals monthly . . .

The most logical goal-setting period is an annual one,
preferably corresponding to the company's fiscal year. While
goal setting should be done yearly, performance ratings
against those goals should be made monthly.

If goals are not reviewed monthly, the end result could be
disaster. If the goal is easier to accomplish than first en-
visioned, the subordinate who sees it within easy reach may
have little incentive to continue working. Conversely, an
employee may be so discouraged by an overambitious goal
as to give up trying entirely.

An analogy might be drawn to the long baseball season:
The runaway team can become lazy; the teams already out
of the running may become disgusted and lethargic. The
only teams playing their hearts out are those who have a

fighting chance at reaching their goal . . . the championship. *Take note, Bowie Kuhn!*

The monthly benchmark meetings to review the goal of the subordinate then naturally coincide with the monthly performance reviews or ratings.

Tell it like it is . . .

Performance rating is a much misunderstood and often poorly handled tool of management. Even if the fairest-of-the-fair personnel form is put into the hands of a manager to rate his subordinates, he is likely either to bend over backward to be a good guy (monotonously checking off "excellent in this; excellent in that" in a useless exercise), or to prove by his illogical nit-picking that he is truly the curmudgeon his subordinates suspected he was.

In the world of performance reviews, subordinates are like students who want a fair report card. They don't particularly want an "easy" teacher whose courses are a snap and who gives them all A's whether they deserve them or not; nor do they want a teacher whose favoritism toward certain classmates shows up on the report cards. They don't want to be teacher's pets, but they don't wish to be class goats either. Your subordinates want a fair evaluation, reflecting their honest performance.

Some companies utilize an annual performance review form; employees are either all rated in the same month, or more or less individually on their hire date or birthday. The form in most current use seems devilishly designed to permit the superior who finds it hard to talk to subordinates to rate them in the solitude of his or her office, and then hand each person the *fait accompli*. Such a form usually contains three spaghetti-wide lines in which the subordinate can present his or her case, should he disagree with the assessment.

These annual performance reviews or ratings are worthless to the company, the superior, and the subordinates. Hastily relegated to the personnel office, they are surreptitiously stacked in some inaccessible corner file. The ratings are an opiate of the masses and of little use in the real world of promotions and salary increases.

Your subordinates want grades or ratings, and they want them monthly! They want your time and attention, your evaluation and assistance, and merited opportunities if they reach or surpass their goals.

Develop a system to treat them fairly,
relative to one another . . .

A good rating system is useful in evaluating subordinates fairly:

> Highest grade: Distinguished Performance (A)
> Next highest: Exceeded Goals (B)
> Next: Fully Met Goals (C)
> Next: Partially Met Goals (D)
> Last: Unsatisfactory Performance (F)

The department head of a major company who used this rating system found the morale of his subordinates so excellent and their motivation so productive within the year that every employee became, in his eyes and their own, *distinguished*. At his expense he bought them all silver lapel pins bearing the number 10, indicating they were the "best." His employees wore the emblems proudly.

The "10's," a point of pride and increased motivation among his employees, became a matter of envy among other employees, including the chief executive officer who asked for one. The department head brashly turned down his boss, standing on the principle that "I really have no way of knowing that your performance is distinguished." (Latest reports indicate they are both still in their positions.)

Goal setting and performance reviews are excellent motivators for your subordinates if handled properly and monthly and *personally*. Do not let the personnel department take over functions with your subordinates that you should be handling. Your interest in these activities shows your subordinates that you are treating them fairly relative to each other. By so doing, you are leading them.

A NOTE OF CAUTION

The analogy between a family and an organization might prompt some enthusiasts to apply the same goal-setting techniques at home, but imposing this discipline on your personal life can cost you the joy of spontaneity. Your homelife may lose some moments of wonder and surprise if you draw up a flow chart on when to buy a new house, the spacing of your children, the purchase of your new car, the morning you will next serve up blueberry pancakes and sausages, or the exact moment you will tell your spouse of your love.

Many management consultants would disagree with the previous sentence, but a number of sociologists agree. Professors Ramon Oldenburg and Dennis Brissett wrote in a recent article: "Our society is impoverished by overcommitment to work and purpose. Each of us runs on too tight a schedule with a predictable world."

Sociologist Richard Sennett concurs: "People suffocate from lack of the new and unexpected, the diverse in their lives."

OTHER MOTIVATORS

Goal setting and performance reviews are two effective motivators, but other factors also motivate people in the workplace. Frederick Herzberg at the University of Utah cites five basic motivators which he calls "satisfiers":

1. The work itself;
2. Responsibility;
3. Achievement;
4. Recognition;
5. Advancement.

The goals program outlined in this chapter can provide motivators by assigning responsibility, measuring achievement, and giving recognition. The work itself and advancement depend on the individual situation.

AND DEMOTIVATORS

Professor Herzberg points out that there are certain obstacles to motivation which he terms "dissatisfiers":

1. Poor company policies and administration;
2. Poor interpersonal relationships with superiors and peers;
3. Inadequate technical supervision;
4. Poor working conditions;
5. Problems in workers' personal lives.

Examples of all five of these dissatisfiers are legion in the workplace in one form or another. They are scramblers of ambition, barriers to fairness, subverters of ethics, and detriments to good business, but they have wide acceptance in the world of commerce.

Demotivating with the annual bonus . . .

An additional dissatisfier, largely unrecognized except by the most knowledgeable and politically aware managers, carries the name of "annual bonus." There are two kinds of bonuses: the "incentive" or "undeserved" bonus and the "under-budget" or "award for a job cheaply done" bonus.

An "incentive bonus" is given to the mall manager at the Snail Darter Plaza, who earns a reward for keeping all the stores constantly filled. When he has a choice between taking on Daddy's Yummy Yogurt, a leisurely growing slow-food chain, right now, or the classier, busier boutique, Le Coq & Les Chickens, four months from now, he opts for the immediacy of the yogurt franchise. He not only gets the bonus from his company for keeping the mall filled, but possibly even a few extra yummies from Daddy's.

The "under-budget bonus" is given to the manager who brings the construction job in under budget, thus sharing in the savings to the company. He doesn't share in the sorrows of the owners, however, who discover some years later that the $50,000 savings on cement to the builder is now costing them $500,000 plus three million in lawsuits from victims of the falling gargoyles.

Anyone who works for such a mall-manipulator manager soon learns his technique for dishonesty, and either follows his example or becomes rapidly demotivated working for him.

The "incentive bonus" is a strange and elusive demotivator. First of all, the company is divided into "bonus-eligible," and "nonbonus-eligible" personnel. If you are on salary and make pretty good money, you are, according to this demotivator, eligible for more. If you don't make pretty good money, you are per se not eligible for any more.

Usually the methodology for carving or hacking out portions from the corporate bonus pie is a closely kept secret. Here is one oft-repeated scenario: The chairman of the board, the president, and the executive vice-president, or some of the above, sit as a bonus committee. They are provided with their own sense of power and greed as well as with lists of all executives making $25,000 or more. The rule of thumb for bonuses is "The less you make, the less you get —even if you are bonus-eligible." Percentage of salary is usually the magic key to the harum-scarum division of corporate spoils.

The First Act of the bonus committee, known as The Skim, is to determine how much each committee member will receive.

For their Second Act the committee proceeds to the lists of executives and decrees bonuses for vice-presidents and some lesser lights, using the percentage methodology.

Act Three is a pompous Revue of the "Indicia of Performance" of the executives under consideration: Does he come to work on time? Is he a liberal? Is he liked by his employees? Is he divorced? Does he play golf? What kind of car does he drive, foreign or domestic?

On such evidence a name is scratched off the list or given the beaming approval of the men in their Santa Claus suits. Woe to you if you weren't—or they *thought* you weren't—a good company boy!

The word "incentive" means to "encourage, rouse, or move to action" or to "motivate in a particular direction." In business or industry, presumably this means a drive to improve performance or production in the coming year. A joyous majority of those clutching mystery checks to their bosoms right after Christmas or New Year's regard them as rewards for jobs well done in the year just past.

The accounts of six different executives who were fired from their jobs a week after receiving their incentive bonuses support the premise that superiors often think of "incentive" as something already accomplished rather than a spur to future achievements.

BONUSES DEMOTIVATE THE BONUS-ELIGIBLE

An even more remarkable disclosure drawn from conversations with both groups of employees is that *the bonus proved more of a demotivator to the bonus-eligible than to the nonbonus-eligible.*

The noneligible, upon mentally accepting the discriminatory company caste system, were content to be paid a living wage; they were not particularly envious of those nervously awaiting their annual dole of the carrot whose size and succulence depended on the whims and prejudices of a few key executives at corporate.

A considerable number of bonus-eligible employees routinely spend, mentally or actually, the annual bonanza before its receipt and face many problems in the year when the well dries up.

A salary plus bonus equals minus what? . . .

If you have a key executive you'd like to keep, be aware that he could be lured away because of the general conviction that "bonus isn't part of salary." He might be making $25,000 a year with you, plus an *almost guaranteed* $5,000 bonus. If the outside company who wants his expertise asks him how much he makes, he'll invariably say $25,000. They might woo him away for $28,000 and *not* give him a bonus.

Employees who are receiving a reasonable wage will no longer be motivated simply by a raise or a bonus; that is usually expected for their staying in the job another year.

A program will motivate when it rewards the achievement of goals previously agreed upon by both organization and employee. The most effective compensation programs combine adequate benefits and salaries across the board with strong employee-relations programs.

Such a program is decidedly more targeted on motivation, improved employee morale, and increased productivity than all the incentive bonuses in the world.

"It's Sunday, children, and we have to look our best."

One company, in its misunderstanding of motivation, promotes an ongoing dress-and-grooming competition. It gently counsels its management team that high-fashion attire is the distinguishing mark of its employees.

The employees, from the top executives down to the most underpaid file clerks, are encouraged to sport the latest fashions as seen in *The New York Times, Vogue, Playboy,* and *The New Yorker,* with the understanding that "It isn't seemly to wear the same outfit more than two days a month."

Have they ever stopped to think what this "Sunday at Our House" routine does for the morale and the pocketbooks of their employees?

The personnel director of another company became annoyed at the informality of dress of some of the women employees. He issued a dress-code directive which clearly spelled out his wishes:

> From now on, there will be no dungarees, slacks, or slack suits worn by the women employees. Dresses, blouses, and skirts will be the attire.

Audrey, a competent and respected executive active in the Equal Rights Movement, arrived at work the next day in a sheer blouse, as required; a skirt, as required; and no undergarments, as they had not been required.

The dress code was quickly amended and then revoked.

> [Men's and] Women's styles may change
> But their designs remain the same.
> —OSCAR WILDE

In summary . . .

This chapter outlines a formula to satisfy the subordinate's needs to be treated *equally among his own peers* and to be *recognized by the superior* (parent figure) for high performance.

Both needs can be facilitated by sensitive and honest performance evaluations based on an achievable—and agreed-upon—set of goals.

Avoid the plague of bonuses, and you may be able to pay higher salaries. If your company insists on a bonus program, remember that bonus time is low morale time and, consequently, low productivity time.

The past three chapters have drawn parallels between organizations and families; subordinates and children. Children and subordinates share the need to be treated fairly, relative to and among each other. Subordinates who are treated fairly will help you do a better job, and you will be leading them. When the time comes for you to move on to better things, they'll be supporting your progress.

HOW TO LEAD:

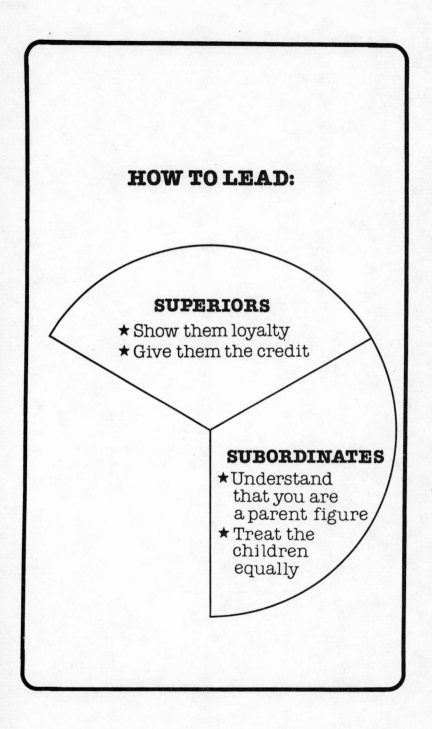

SUPERIORS
★ Show them loyalty
★ Give them the credit

SUBORDINATES
★ Understand that you are a parent figure
★ Treat the children equally

Part Four. HOW TO LEAD PEERS

Chapter 9. KNOWING WHAT THEY WANT AND GETTING IT FOR THEM

First say to yourself what you would be; and then do what you have to do . . .

—EPICTETUS

Earlier in the book you analyzed your own company or corporate structure, established where you stood on the ladder, and identified your superiors, subordinates, and peers. You have already learned much about how to lead your subordinates . . . and your superiors.

In this chapter you will learn how to determine what your peers want from their jobs and their lives. *Knowing* what they want will put you on the road to *leading* them. Peers are defined as equals, of course, but, as is true in many other areas of apparent equality, some are more equal than others.

Your peers are the hardest group to lead because you are competing with them for a decreasing number of rungs on the organizational ladder.

If you can assess their wants and then position yourself to satisfy these wants, your peers will give you leadership so as not to lose your favor and, ultimately, your favors.

Before outlining and illustrating the recommended political methodology on *How to Lead Peers,* it seems appropriate to point out again that survival and success are both desirable and legitimate goals in your life; and to stress once more that the technique outlined here is neither Machiavellian nor unethical.

Leo Durocher is credited with pronouncing, "Nice guys finish last." You can be "nice" and still finish first. Being nice conflicts in no way with following the recommended techniques to lead your peers.

Why is it so important to lead your peers? It comes down to this: *Before you can be promoted, your peers often must agree to follow you.* If you are considered for a promotion which would make you the superior of your present peers, they will have to accept this organizational change. They will probably be asked: "Would you like to work for this man (or woman)?" Their responses to your possible promotion might be elicited in a less direct fashion, but they will be consulted. You do not want their reply to be "I would *never* work for that so-and-so!"

If you have already been *leading* your peers in a manner they would like to continue, you're on your way!

It's not easy; you're a rival . . .

Of the three groups of coworkers you must lead to advance your career, your peers are the most difficult. By the nature of your organizational equality, you are a threat to their advancement and, therefore, to their image and their psyche.

As our chapter heading indicates, *your initial course of action in leading your peers is to know what they want!*

Sound simple? It's not so simple, but it's not impossible. Learning what each peer *really* wants requires lots of homework on your part, a serious study of human nature, much questioning and listening and observing, and maybe even a two-martini lunch occasionally.

To start . . .

Start with a simple notebook to launch your scientific analysis of peer politics. This is your *inventory notebook*. Answer the questions listed below—without guilt—about *each* of your peers. If you don't know the answers, you can probably find them out by simply listening to and observing your peers closely. The questions are not all-inclusive, but will give you an idea of how to approach this important stage in the advancement of your career.

1. What does he or she want from his or her current job?
2. What job does this person eventually want in the organization?
3. What is the state of his or her personal life? What satisfactions seem to be missing that he or she may be seeking at work instead of at home?
4. Does he or she have hobbies, and if so, what are they?
5. What is his or her relationship to peers? superiors? subordinates?

Your inventory notebook should be similar to the following example.

Bill Duke, Chief of Finance:

Bill is fish-cold, defensive, sensitive personally yet insensitive to the feelings of others. He is a logical leader, whose tight ship resembles the *Bounty*. He came to the company ten years ago from a bank in Chicago, where he was the lending officer with the highest percentage of loan turndowns in history. Bill feels that he is capable of assuming the top position in The Company but is convinced that he is not a favored son or protégé of his superior.

He apparently does, however, have his eyes on the "main chance" in Finance at the corporate office. His chances there depend on attrition as well as the professionalism of his P & L (profit and loss) statements and on the manner in which he controls unnecessary expenses.

He seems to have a fixation on even slightly inflated expense accounts—as though they were a greater threat to the company's financial stability than an ill-advised and chancy research and development project.

Bill has been married for twenty-two years; the children have taken off for careers and freedoms in California. The Dukes feel they have decently and adequately performed the expected parental rites of bringing up their offspring through college, but they get little tangible return on this investment besides an occasional picture of the grandchildren gamboling on Fisherman's Wharf.

Bill took up pitch-and-putt and driving-range golf five years ago, when he discovered that a well-hit little white ball can relieve some of the frustrations of business. He is now breaking ninety, and his club membership (for which he pays, unlike some of his peers who claim golf as a sales tool) and his Christmas gift set of clubs have taken on a position of growing importance in his life.

Many of Bill's peers and their subordinates, because of the nature of their positions, often travel far and first-class on company business; he is jealous of their freedom and "the good times they have on company money." He often mentions that The Company's business could do just as well without all this hopscotching of marketing, public relations and engineering personnel. He enviously wonders what they do at night in fancy hotels so far from home.

Bill is an extremely competent Chief of Finance. He meets twice a month with his superior and logically sets down the current and projected fiscal picture with appropriate charts and terse commentary. But even in the case of his boss, Bill's insensitivity and expense-account mania get him into deep water. The Boss's secretary recalls the following incident:

The Boss had an important (and, as it turned out, fruitful) business meeting in San Francisco. His secretary obtained his first-class plane ticket, plus a thousand-dollar advance. When the Boss returned, he handed his secretary all his hotel bills, meal stubs, and car-rental payments, plus the cash remaining from the "advance" . . . $62.60. It was up to her to fill in the blanks on the travel and expense statement totaling $937.40. This was sent to the office of Chief of Finance with the $62.60 in cash.

During a reporting session with the Boss a few days later, in an effort to flaunt his thoroughness, Bill grinned knowingly. "You must have had a great time in San Francisco, Boss."

"How did you know, Duke?" he responded abruptly.

"I—uh—just happened to notice your expense account, Boss," Bill said as sheepishly as a Basset hound can be sheepish.

Bill has never quite gotten the egg off his face.

Read back through the inventory of Bill Duke and try to analyze what he *really wants*. If you learn that, and he can sense that *you know what he wants, you have already begun to lead him.*

Bill will *never* get what he wants until he changes the way he treats those with whom he works. He is a completely apolitical animal.

Bill Duke wants:

1. To change his boss's perception of him. He knows he won't get promoted if he doesn't.

2. To find out exactly what he does that the Boss doesn't like.

3. To do more business travel and enjoy himself more.

4. To have more time to play golf.

Here is another example of a peer inventory:

Suzy Viscount, Chief of Promotions and Public Relations:
Suzy is twenty-six. She is a graduate of the Missouri School of Journalism. After graduation she spent three years as a

junior copywriter at an advertising agency in New York. She was hired six months ago by The Company and reports to the Boss and to the Director of Public Relations and Advertising at the corporate office.

Suzy and her secretary work together as a skilled team. Although the first two weeks of their association were a little strained, Suzy soon proved her professionalism to her secretary, to her superior, and to Bill Duke, with whom she interacted on her budgeting and expense control.

She has had little contact with her peers. She is, however, most anxious to familiarize herself with all areas of The Company, "as it differs widely in organization and procedure from the advertising agency."

Suzy rented an apartment in a high-rise just beyond the borders of the town; if its decor resembles her office, it is quiet and comfortable and reflects her good taste. Two of her own watercolor originals grace her office: one, a peaceful scene of a red barn in Vermont; the other, a sympathetic view of faces on a Lexington Avenue subway. You know of no one in The Company who has visited Suzy at home.

When she first joined The Company, she was a slightly lost babe in a new woods. In answer to her questions you told her as much as you knew about how Promotions and Public Relations had been handled in the past (very unimaginatively), and indicated that you felt she could do a more competent job than her predecessor, a former newspaperman of suspect drinking habits who confused press agentry with public relations. His proudest accomplishment was when he got his superior's name in a gossip column: The item bordered on the slanderous and sensational, and the hunt was on for a new chief.

Suzy wonders why she was chosen for the job as chief. She had learned that there were three prime candidates for the position, all about equal in the quality of their résumés, portfolios, and references, and the Boss, in concurrence with the corporate Director of Public Relations and Advertising, picked her.

Suzy has a written five-year plan.

She confides that she would like to spend about five years with The Company and then move up to corporate in the Public Relations and Advertising Department.

After reviewing your inventory of Suzy you conclude that her intentions are not exactly as she describes them. Her real aspirations are not with this company at all. You deduce that on her last job with the ad agency her career was blocked from advancing. People of her caliber rarely remain as junior copywriters for more than a year or so. When you researched the ad agency she left, you learned it had come upon hard times along with the rest of the industry about a year earlier. What Suzy wants is:

1. To connect with a prestigious advertising agency, magazine, or public relations firm as soon as better times return to the advertising field.

2. To receive an outstanding performance appraisal by the Boss for use with her résumé.

3. To have no long-range ties with anyone in The Company.

4. To go back to New York.

5. To hide her real intentions.

Once your inventory on peers is completed, you will know much more than you did about the obvious and partially hidden wants of your peers, and you can assist them in *getting what they want.* By so doing, you will be helping them as well as helping yourself!

A note of caution: The office is not the place . . .

Regarding homework: Do your mental work, as well as your questioning, listening, and observing, in the office or on the road or in the neighborhood restaurant. But for the sake of harmony, work on your *peer inventory and analysis* at home. There are those who can read a colleague's writing upside down or make damaging assumptions from a hazy photo copy spotted in the wastebasket.

PRIORITIZE NEEDS

How do you go about getting for them what they want? The first step is to *prioritize* the needs of your peers. The *XABC System* is probably the best method to organize both your personal and business life:

X = Urgent; drop everything until this is done.
A = Highest importance, but not urgent.
B = Medium-high importance, but can wait a while.
C = Low importance; can wait indefinitely.

Using this system, determine the X needs of your peers from the inventories you've compiled. You are then in a position to assess the best way to help each satisfy his or her X need, whether he or she knows of it or not.

Do not worry about the A needs of your peers until you have taken care of the X for all of them. Only then do you begin to work down the list—and this will be easier—on everyone's A; everyone's B; everyone's C.

OPEN A ROUNDHOUSE

Capitalizing on your status as a peer, now is the time for you to open your Roundhouse, or confessional, for business. It may not pay to advertise, but you should get the word around.

A roundhouse is a circular railroad enginehouse built on a turntable. It is used to repair trains and put them back on the right tracks. Your office can become the Roundhouse of your organization: *Come unto me, all you peers who want to talk about your problems and get your trains of thought pointed in the right directions, and I will talk away your troubles. Business hours, 3 to 6 P.M. daily at my Round-*

house. Special appointments at Milhaly's Happy Hour Saloon, 6 to 9 P.M., just before Monday night baseball or football or bingo.

Your initial task is to assure your peers' comfort in entering the Roundhouse and confiding their concerns so that you can change their oil or repair their slipping clutches or polish their rusty wheels. You can learn to repair their hurts, pump up their egos and set them straight just by talking over ways they can deal with their superior or the other peers.

To get your show on the road, you may have to lug the Roundhouse to their office retreats where they huddle sulking in the corner. If your advice is gently to the point and your problem-solving suggestions are straightforward and useful, they will be driving their trains to your Roundhouse before you know it.

OPERATING THE ROUNDHOUSE

Let's return now to The Company. For illustration, in the dialogue that follows, you will be "Betty."

The X (Top Priority) of Bill Duke, Chief of Finance:
He wants to change his boss's perception of him.
Betty: Good afternoon, Bill, do you mind if I come in?
Bill: What's the problem, Betty—an expense check slow in coming? Sure, come on in. Would you like coffee?
Betty: Black with sugar. Just one, thanks. No problem, Bill. Four o'clock has always been a low point for me. I feel like sitting down, chatting, and relaxing over coffee with a friend. After fifteen minutes or so, it's gung-ho time again. Don't you ever feel that way?
Bill: Not much. A controller doesn't have many friends— I mean, people you can talk to. I don't recommend approval of their appropriations, and they get mad. I question their expense accounts, and they get mad. They don't get cash ad-

vances processed five minutes after they've applied for them, and they get steamed. They don't appreciate the demands put on this office. They don't realize the pressure the Old Man puts on me. But you don't want to talk about that.

Betty: Sure I do. I happen to get along with the Old Man, but my job isn't as tough as yours. He seems like a nice enough guy. I guess some people just rub him the wrong way. I just came from his office, and he okayed a new copying machine for my department.

Bill: Betty, you know, I'm one of the prime ones who does rub him the wrong way. I don't mean to, but I always seem to be ruffling his feathers. I'm supposed to be watching the cashbox, but if I make a crack about somebody overrunning his appropriation or having a great time in Tampa during a business trip boondoggle, he doesn't like it. Once I thought I was being funny and winked and told him that judging from his expense account, he must have had a great time in San Francisco. He didn't talk to me for two weeks.

Betty: Yeah, I heard.

Bill: Where did you hear?

Betty: His secretary told me. She was sorry for you. The Boss is a sensitive soul, and he's every inch a boss. He doesn't like anybody making cracks on how he does his job. He thinks you sometimes talk before you think.

Bill: I was only kidding. If anybody has a right to stretch his expense account a bit, especially after closing that big sale, he does. If there's one guy in this company really doing his job the way it should be done, it's the Boss.

Betty: Did you ever tell him that? Most people don't know how good they are unless someone tells them. I make it a practice to tell the Boss how well he handles his special accounts.

Bill: I think you're right. Maybe I'll stop trying to be funny and be more careful when I talk to him. Say, drop up again anytime and we'll talk. Or I'll wander down to your office. Where is it, again?

Now on to Suzy Viscount, and in this case you'll be "Barney."

The X of Suzy Viscount, Chief of Public Relations:

Suzy's X want is to receive an outstanding performance appraisal by the boss to use in her résumé. This written rating can also be given to executive employment agencies (headhunters), making her more attractive to potential employers. It will probably mean at least three to five thousand dollars more per year in salary when she negotiates with a new employer.

You visit her office:

Barney: Hello, Suzy!

Suzy: Barney, my first buddy in The Company! What's with you today?

Barney: Well, I had a few minutes to spare and thought I'd use them to tell you something I've been meaning to say for a week or so.

Suzy: Okay, Barney, what is it?

Barney: I think you've been doing one hell of a job since you came with The Company. A good example is the quality of the promotion you did in the Midwest Region promoting our new lines. I told the Boss just that when we were traveling on the plane to St. Louis together a couple of weeks ago. I told him that in my book you deserved no less than an *excellent* rating so far, and if you kept on going at that pace for the whole year, he ought to consider expanding your role into advertising.

Suzy: Hey, wow, Barney! You sure have a way of making a woman feel good. I'll buy you a drink after work.

AFTER ALL THE TOP PRIORITIES ARE COMPLETED

Once you have obtained the X for your peers, their most urgent needs, you are on target. They will all be aware of the assistance you have given them, and *you will be leading them.*

Helping them satisfy their A, B, and C needs from your inventory then becomes relatively easy. The other needs seem to disappear like falling dominoes once the X need is satisfied.

ON BEING A RUMPELSTILTSKIN MANAGER

Briefly, the story of Rumpelstiltskin is about a miller who told the King that his daughter could turn straw into gold. He was just making conversation, but the King put the daughter in a room with a little bit of straw and commanded her to turn it into gold. She couldn't and began to cry.

This is where Rumpelstiltskin entered the story. He told the miller's daughter that he would change the straw into gold for a locket, which he did.

Delighted, the King put her in a bigger room with more straw. Again she cried, and again Rumpelstiltskin came. This time she gave him her bracelet, and he changed the straw into gold.

The greedy King put her in a bigger room with more straw, but she had nothing left to give Rumpelstiltskin. He offered to turn the straw into gold if she gave her first baby to him. She said "yes," and he again turned the straw into gold. The King asked for her hand in marriage, and later, when they had a baby, guess who came a-callin'?

Rumpelstiltskin, of course!

He demanded the baby according to their agreement—unless she could guess his name in three days. She discovered that it was Rumpelstiltskin and kept the baby. Rumpelstiltskin stamped so hard in anger that he sank into the earth and was never heard from again.

Using political skills you can turn your peers' straw into gold. . . .

Once your office has become a Roundhouse for assisting your peers, you will find yourself in much the same position as Rumpelstiltskin. Your peers will continually seek your assistance as the miller's daughter sought Rumpelstiltskin's.

She needed the straw to be turned into gold, and he could do it. Through the use of your political skills, you will be able to take the straw brought to you by your peers and turn it into gold—a feat for which they will undoubtedly feel appreciative and indebted to you.

For example, suppose a peer brings you a report for management on which he or she has been working for some time. You see that the issues involved are perfectly stated but that the method of presentation puts top management in a bad light for ignoring the situation so long. The report could be symbolically referred to as straw, for it will never be implemented.

With your magic political touch, you can lead your peer, convincing him or her to rework the report so that it does not offend anyone. The merit of the report's logical ideas can be seen by all who read it, and because of your input the valuable contents will not be emotionally discarded by management. You have thus changed straw into gold. You can be sure that your peer will soon be calling on you again to weave your magic.

Suppose that on another occasion your peer is writing up a request for a new piece of equipment for his department. He or she doubts the request will be granted because the Boss has been on a cost-cutting drive for the past few weeks, even though the new machine will save money in the long run and make the whole department run more smoothly right away.

You suggest that the request include a recommendation that the equipment be ordered from a competitively priced supplier to whom you know the Boss owes a favor. The request is granted, and you have again turned a peer's straw into gold.

CHANGE THE STORY'S ENDING

You will be doing favors for your peers while helping them achieve their objectives. As you weave your magic and their gold, do not ask for too much in return. Seek only a quid pro quo; no more. You may choose to save the favors your peers owe you until you are in a position to achieve one of your X wants. Then cash in as many chips as necessary to get what you want. But be light-footed; don't come on so strong that they hear the stamp of your foot and arrange for you to sink into the earth!

FOR MY FIRST WISH . . .

Things are proceeding very well. Following the lead of Betty and Barney, you have *determined* your peers' wants and have begun to take steps to help them achieve their objectives. Your first step was to prioritize each peer's needs. You then made your office a Roundhouse to connect various trains or lend an understanding ear, depending on what was required.

Your supportiveness has earned you chips which you could call on if you wanted something from your peers. Because you have been cautious not to use your chips wantonly, you have retained enough of them to make the big move to get yourself promoted.

. . . IF I COULD BE WHATEVER I WANT

By now you are probably looking at things from a political perspective, so you ask yourself, "Which positions in organizational life carry political advantages? Disadvantages?"

When your boss begins to talk about your taking on additional duties—after you have planted the seed with one of your beholden peers, knowing he or she would mention it to the Boss—what are you going to strike for?

The captain at sea or in the air, or the astronaut hurtling through space, reports his *position*; the government takes a *position* vis-à-vis another nation; the baseball player fields several *positions*; the nobleman inherited his *position*; and the unwary executive may lose his *position*.

Position is not everything, but it is a lot. *Position* can be defined as the way a thing or person is placed in relation to other things or persons. For our purposes it is more accurately defined as the spot, place, or condition *that gives one the advantage over another.*

Consider some of the power centers in the medium-to-large company or organization. It is unlikely that you will ever control more than a handful of these departments or functions as you begin your ascent to the top. But the control of one or two or three, either directly or through a faithful subordinate, will give you enough leverage to *get for your peers what they want.*

1. Personnel Department

As Director of Personnel, you may advise on or control salary ranges in all echelons of management; advise on or control employee selection for new jobs or old ones vacated by attrition; control the benefits program; and expedite medical and insurance claims.

Even though you must be wary in this department of occasionally being considered disloyal to The Company because you can't ram an unpopular management decision down the throats of the employees, Personnel is still a considerable power center.

Labor Relations is an enormously important field. As you find yourself dealing with union officials and taking a leading company role in negotiations for a new contract, your importance to the company and your standing with your peers will inevitably increase. You'll be talking to the Controller about the union's financial demands, and to the Director of Sales to suggest that he and his contracts people not make any firm price or delivery commitments until negotiations are settled.

You will find yourself talking to the Director of Public Relations, and making him an integral adjunct to the negotiating team. You will keep him continually and thoroughly updated on the progress of negotiations. If you and the union agree on a media blackout, he can either take the night off or drink Black Russians in the bar of the hotel where you are meeting with the union.

You will be talking to the Director of Engineering. All he needs is to have his hand held.

Sometimes, too, in negotiating with a union which is doing a good job for its members but is giving you ulcers, you will find that you are talking to yourself.

2. Purchasing Department

The streams of eager and young, middle-aged and polished, old and desperate salesmen trudging their way to the lobbies of the purchasing departments in this country would triangulate nicely from Portland, Oregon, to Dallas, Texas, and back to New York. And over and over again.

"Mr. Sampson, here to see Ms. Oswald. My company has a new system for storing old files or filing old stores."

Ms. Oswald, a smart purchasing buyer or director, can make points with her peers by the way she handles their requests for supplies, equipment, and vital material. If she is sharp enough to anticipate her peers' desires and, for example, puts a new wine-colored rug in the Controller's office over the weekend (she knew from the moneyman's wife that he liked the color), she has stored up Brownie points for herself in her campaign for recognition and promotion by her peers.

And when the bill for the wine-colored rug reaches the Controller, it will be quietly approved . . . as will other bills of a less extravagant nature submitted by the office of the Director of Purchasing.

Ms. Oswald stops by one of her peers' offices and reconnoiters the furniture. The couch springs are reaching hungrily for the indoor-outdoor rug, which looks as though it spent most of its life outdoors.

She immediately orders the makings of a dream office from her new furniture budget "cushion" (born in the glow of the Controller's wine-colored rug), and the peer is most grateful for her purchases and promptness.

3. Controller's Department

Nicknames for the controller of any company range from "Scrooge," "that tight-fisted bastard," and "that sneaky son of a bitch" to less flattering descriptions. Controllers seem universally unpopular. They are withal a strange and successful breed, these keepers of the bottom line, for the bottom line is the god of the western world.

Visualize yourself as the Controller. What other arrows of fortune do you have in your quiver?

* You decide who will get company credit cards.

* You decide who will get travel advances . . . and how much.

* You decide (unless there is a company policy based on rank) who will fly first-class and who will go down in the galley and help row.

* You decide whose expense accounts slide through without a whimper and whose will be scrutinized for the slightest deviation from reality:

"Do you have a receipt, Fitzsimmons, for this thirty-cent tip to the Washington taxi driver?"

"No, sir, but I do have a black eye."

Controllers have a position in The Company which, if handled with skill, could be the most powerful political center of all.

4. The Accounting Function

In most companies the Accounting Function, which includes Accounts Receivable, reports to the Controller. It is by itself a power center, however. The Accounting Department can control the figures to make a proposal or project look good or disastrous. You can cater to a peer by bending the flexible numbers in his or her direction; or you can thwart him or her by nudging the numbers in the opposite direction.

From Accounts Payable you can control who gets his money first. This determines the happy suppliers on whom you can depend to deliver promised goods or services when needed:

"Wilbur, I just paid the bill from the Molten Steel Conglomerate right on time. If you want them in a hurry again, I'm sure they'll pour right over. Ha-ha."

"Gee whiz, thanks, Edgar, you're a brick."

The more people and peers who think you're a brick, the better.

5. *Computer Operations*

The computer is "magic world" to most executives, who have only a passing knowledge of its mysterious workings. "Garbage in, garbage out," they spout knowingly when they meet with the Director of Computer Operations, winking to indicate their ignorance.

If you find yourself in charge of the computer operations of your company, what do you do first?

"Johnson, I guess you've heard that I have been put in charge of computer operations."

Johnson says he's heard a lot about you and it's all good. (He'd used the same line on his previous four bosses, receiving immediate salary increments in each case retroactive to the day of the compliment.)

You learn that Johnson has been under pressure from all departments for more programming time, and now the pressure shifts to you. Each of your peers needs "runoffs" for this or that purpose: payroll checks (most important!), wage and salary comparisons, sales projections, product analyses, and industry statistics of all kinds. You discover that with the addition of two keypunch operators and one experienced programmer, you can satisfy all your peers.

Because you know how to lead your superiors, you are granted an increase in the computer operations budget to hire the new people. You satisfy your peers' wants. They like you. You have a tight and rewarding control of a power center, and you are leading them.

6. *Public Relations*

Most people were born with a fascination for seeing their pictures in the paper and their names in print. Your peers aren't likely to call on you to take their pictures and write releases on their latest trips, professional awards, or honors for community work. But they will greet you with open arms and well-ordered information if *you* take the initiative. Your plant newspaper offers an excellent platform for ingratiating yourself with your peers:

"We are starting a new feature in the company paper next month, Miss Winsome. It's called 'Department of the Month.' The department head will be featured, with emphasis on his or her dedication and responsibilities, difficulties, and triumphs. I expect to get some inspiring quotes from you! I'd like a picture of you at the blackboard explaining strategy to your staff, and another of you dictating to your secretary."

This moment of glory brings Winsome under your spell. The remainder of your peers excitedly anticipate their moment in the sun as "The Department of . . ."

Although the profession of public relations is far more than publicity, it is primarily viewed this way by the general public and your peers. Howard Hughes once hired one of the most prestigious public relations counselors in the country, the late Carl Byoir, to keep his name *out* of the papers; you may at some time be called on to do the same thing.

The Public Relations Department may be responsible for preparing slide presentations for departments in need of them. Your sales and marketing peers may want video cassette presentations or flip charts or charts of many colors. So may Personnel. Or Engineering. Or Manufacturing. When you produce a professional job for them in a timely manner, you are a peer they can trust—a peer they can follow.

7. *The Office Manager*

In certain companies or branch offices thereof, this is a significant, if highly underrated, power center. You control office allocation: who gets the window facing the park; who gets the parking spot near the front of the lot; and many other highly treasured benefits.

This is a partial list of power centers which will vary with each organization. Begin looking at the power centers in yours. Do an analysis of each department to determine the relative political merits of each.

Prepare to position yourself *strategically* in a politically potent area of your organization from which you can make peers purr happily in your direction.

"But what about the rest of my peers?" you ask. "Won't they be planning the same strategy? Won't they be out to control these same centers of power within my company? They're not dopes, you know!"

They're obviously not dopes, since they have attained a job on the level with yours. Thoughtful observation should assure you, however, that most people bumble along, naïvely waiting for the big break. Some merely sit on the stool at the soda fountain, hoping to be discovered.

Many apparent tigers are pussycats, and many shepherds are more nearly sheep. And many others whose innate wisdom should rank them as serious contenders lack the perseverance to achieve their goals.

In summary . . .

One definition for the word "rival" is "peer." An obscure definition is "a companion in duty."

When you seek a promotion as "one of two or more striving for what only one can possess," you are again a rival.

So even by definition, peers are rivals, "striving for competitive advantage." Given the nature of this association, it is no small feat to win the support of your peers. But their support you must have, because they will surely be polled as to whether they will follow you if you are promoted.

On a logical level they may resent your promotion because they are thereby denied it. On an emotional level they may be as jealous as siblings are of each other's advantages. You should, therefore, be leading them already by meeting so many of their needs that they are afraid not to support you.

If you are feeding their most important needs, they will be reluctant to bite your hand.

This chapter describes the process of learning to lead your peers by getting for them what they want. To accomplish this, first develop an inventory of wants for your peers and prioritize their needs.

The Roundhouse is an effective method for learning about and advising your peers. Get them in the Roundhouse and talk sense with them; change their oil and perspectives and move them out on the right tracks. Establishing the Roundhouse gives you a framework in which you can meet their needs. If you succeed, you will lead them.

When your turn to achieve an X want arrives, you will

be in a strong position to call on your peers for their help. Before deciding on your next position, however, do a careful analysis to determine the power centers in your organization. Look for politically strong areas from which you can continue to meet the needs of your peers as well as your own.

HOW TO LEAD:

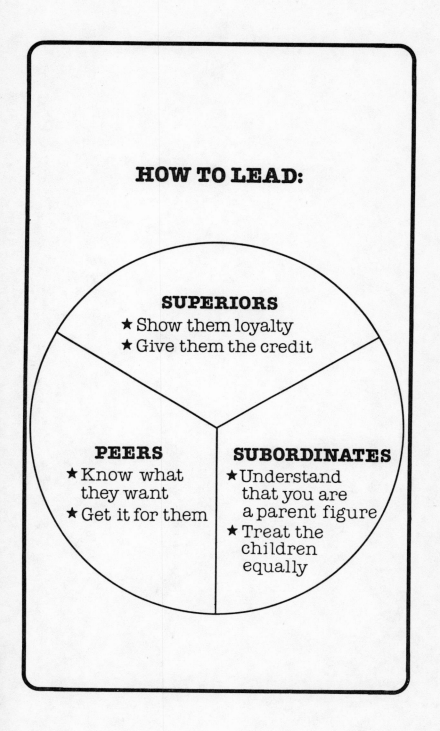

SUPERIORS
★ Show them loyalty
★ Give them the credit

PEERS
★ Know what they want
★ Get it for them

SUBORDINATES
★ Understand that you are a parent figure
★ Treat the children equally

Part Five. SOME GENERAL POLITICAL TOOLS

Chapter 10. WHEN TO TALK

"Really, now you ask me," said Alice,
". . . I don't think—"
"Then you shouldn't talk," said the Hatter.
—LEWIS CARROLL

Imagine what a quiet place the world would be if everyone in the business—and social—world followed the sound advice of the Hatter! And if thought preceded talk, far less ignorance, egotism, or naïveté would be apparent.

That maxim is all well and good until we are *called* upon to speak. We may know it is in our best interests to be quiet and vacate the premises as soon as possible; instinct tells us *nothing* is to be gained by verbalizing *anything*. Yet silence is sometimes not an option.

One solution in this situation is to imitate a football team in trouble: Fall back ten yards and punt! For example, a teacher returned from a meeting shaking her head in disbelief.

"What happened?" I asked.

"At the start of the meeting," she explained, "the principal handed out the agenda for the day: seven items, typed on white paper and copied on the machine in his office. Before the meeting started, the usual ten minutes late, we had time to read the agenda, drink our coffee, and enjoy brownies cooked by the freshman Home-Ec class.

"The principal called the meeting to order, checked the roll, and then read the agenda to us. He actually read it!

Half of the teachers at the meeting have master's degrees in English, and he read us a seven-line agenda! All short words. Like 'home room,' 'study hall,' 'graduation,' 'conduct,' 'tests,' 'cocaine,' and 'sex behind the bleachers.' That took fifteen minutes. Then we went down the list on the agenda, and as he came to each item he would read it again. Twice. I need a drink!"

I asked her if she had shared with the principal her feelings about his handling of the meeting.

"I was tempted to tell him what a horrible meeting he ran," she confessed, "but I resisted. I could have said it was a great meeting, but that would have been too dishonest. I settled for telling him that the time certainly went by during the meeting. If he presumed I meant it went by swiftly, that's as dishonest as I care to be. And I still have my nicely tenured job."

The teacher was no Alice, and the Hatter would have been proud of her performance. She knew when to talk and what to say. The subordinate cannot be completely candid in a world where most superiors are thin-skinned. The silent and approving yes-man or woman has a greater chance for survival than the individual who feels he owes it to his inner peace to tell it like it is.

A sad reality is that there is simply no reward for honesty in most human interactions.

Although people often ask our opinions, imploring us to be honest even if it hurts, it is rare that anyone really wants to hear anything negative about himself. Such honesty may, in fact, destroy or seriously damage a relationship.

The mother of a girl who was being bullied at school asked a male coworker what she could do about it. His instincts told him the woman didn't really want to know but sought reassurance that she was a good mother. He knew the bullied daughter was afraid of nearly everything. If he asked her why she feared this or that, she would reply, "Mommy says it can hurt me, so I have to be careful."

He ignored his instincts and told the mother he thought she was being overprotective. He even explained how the child's dependence on the mother left her unable to defend herself against the more aggressive children in the school-yard. This response incensed the mother!

His accurate instincts and honest intentions are little comfort to him against the cold stares of a no-longer-friendly coworker.

"SPEAK UP, GET FIRED"

Talking at the wrong time, or saying the wrong thing, is a sure way of getting yourself fired.

In a *New York Times* article entitled "Speak Up, Get Fired," on Sunday, June 10, 1979, Jack Stieber, a professor of economics and Director of the School of Labor and Industrial Relations at Michigan State University, wrote of the job vulnerability of millions of Americans:

> Assuming that all union members, government employees, and the relatively small number of persons who have individual contracts with their employers are protected against unfair dismissal, that leaves about 30 million wage-and-salary employees in the United States who may be dismissed at any time by their employers for any reason or for no reason.
>
> This distinction between different groups of employees, while taken for granted in the United States, is found in few industrialized countries. Most countries provide some degree of legal protection against unjust dismissal.
>
> Unorganized employees, including supervisors and middle management, who constitute a substantial portion of the United States work force, lack the protection that is accorded by law to all employees in most other countries. There is no rational basis for this distinction.

But the distinction exists. And it will probably continue.

There is reason to suspect that the majority of supervisors and managers who were fired in the United States during the past several years *said the wrong thing to their superiors* or *about their superiors*, or were unable to talk sensibly when the appropriate business occasion arrived.

We must conclude that knowing *when to talk* and *when not to talk* is important not only in one's advance up through the ranks, but is vital to one's survival in the job market. It is difficult to separate advice on *when to talk* and *when not to talk* into easily partitioned slots, because the one activity complements the other inactivity, but we will touch on *when to talk* as the first part of this significant double-header:

As children, we were told not to speak until spoken to.

"How old are you, my little man?" You look the svelte-looking lady in the eye and say, "Seven, Mrs. Larthen, and how old are you?"

"Janet, is there anything the matter?" your teacher asks.

"Yes, Mrs. Insbruck, I just had an accident." Since she doesn't ask further and presumes the usual accident for a seven year old, you don't feel you need to tell her you stubbed your toe.

The soldier taken in combat by the enemy is instructed to give only his name, rank and serial number:

"Charles de Gaulle. Corporal. Six-eight-nine-seven-two-three-one-four-zero."

Not so incidentally, there are twelve words in the above reply. This brings us conveniently to my Theory of the Twelve Words.

Learn to say it in twelve words or less . . .

Following the Theory of the Twelve Words, you boil down your thinking on a subject before speaking so that it streaks out in a twelve-bolt flash of lightning when you finally have the floor. Condense any recommendation for a proposal, problem, or course of action. Be ready with the

Twelve Words that could dispatch the meeting fast, or at least get it off dead center and pointed in the right direction. The Twelve Words will demonstrate your leadership and the fact that you think before you talk.

Forget the extra phrases and frills and fancy embroidery, and take your words to the heart of the matter. Delete "I think"; "I would guess"; "It would appear to me"; "As I was saying just the other day"; and "That reminds me of a story." Strike with the thought-out truth in Twelve Words or less:

"Let's purchase the acre and build the lab there. It's economically sound."

"That advertising agency stressed our product quality and honesty. I'll buy that."

"My study supports every item in the president's proposal. Let's okay it."

> To talk without thinking is to shoot without aiming.
> —THOMAS FULLER, *Gnomologia* (1732)

Although an occasional emergency meeting may be called whose subject is a mystery until the Boss drops the bombshell on his staff, you will usually be aware of the reason for the meeting and may even receive an advance copy of the agenda. If you can contribute to or control the agenda, so much the better.

To utilize the Theory of the Twelve Words, you need a thorough knowledge of the subject at hand, so study the agenda carefully.

Develop a logical—and, if possible, popular—recommendation before you open your mouth. You must be more prepared than anyone else in the room to hit your target with your first Twelve Words.

> *When meeting with your superior,*
> *your ideas are never subordinate . . .*

The "Siddhartha Principle," named for the main character in Hermann Hesse's book of that name, reveals how a subordinate can convey the impression that though subordinate in rank, he or she is not subordinate in ideas. This is important to remember in meeting with your superior.

During preliminary discussion, you need not talk at all. You can subordinate your posture, your body language, and your spoken language, saying "sir," where appropriate. When the discussion turns to the meat of the meeting and ideas, you can change your posture, body language, and verbal approach, acting as a peer or even a superior. Be fully prepared to discuss your ideas, without leaning forward, and then avoid the word "sir."

When you and your subordinates meet
with your superior, you do the talking . . .

Consider the case of Claudine Cleaver, in charge of the company photographic lab. She reports to you and she has proposed an in-house television system. The Boss wants to talk about it. Although your temptation may be to let Claudine do all the talking as well as explain the technical equipment, resist it. You must lead the talking, asking Claudine questions and expounding on the workings of the character generator and the cost of the video cable from the communications center to the main cafeteria and the Boss's office.

Permitting Claudine to carry the whole ball of wax might lead your Boss to think he can meet more efficiently with your subordinates without you. If you contribute nothing of substance to the meeting, even your subordinates may think they can bypass you and have direct access to the Boss.

As with most words of wisdom, these, too, must be kept in perspective. Talking excessively may create the impression to your superior that you are blocking out your subordinates, and may leave your subordinates feeling ineffectual.

When meeting with your subordinates,
talk as little as possible . . .

In their desire to please you, your subordinates will respond to the gentle nudges you give them to move in the direction of the idea or solution you want. At the appropriate moment, when they turn to you for final direction, you can use the Theory of the Twelve Words to confirm the "joint" decision. The key to a successful meeting with your subordinates is to avoid inhibiting them by talking too much.

There will, of course, be occasions when your contribution to meetings goes far beyond the Twelve Words, but brevity is still the byword! Do not let this Lincolnian accusation ever describe your style:

He can compress the most words into the smallest thoughts of any man I ever met.

—ABRAHAM LINCOLN

Give handouts only after the meeting . . .

The Boss's secretary notifies you that he wants you to give a presentation to the rest of the staff on the approved advertising campaign for the coming year. You plan it well. You huddle with the advertising agency and borrow the flip-chart presentation they used in convincing you and your boss and the head of marketing. You utilize the finished artwork and the roughs, and reproduce the schedule of insertions in the various publications. You develop an appropriate summary to hand out to the staff members following your presentation. If you give it to them before you talk, they will leaf through it during your homily like occasional churchgoers looking for the right hymn.

FEEDBACK

The principle of adjusting behavior on the basis of response to past performance is known as *feedback*, a word which has come a long way since first used in correcting the electrical ills of automobiles.

Two important times to talk are when you are giving *positive feedback* and when you are giving *negative feedback*.

Positive Feedback: Almost everyone is starved for positive feedback. People want to hear that they are good at what they are doing, and that their work product is worthy of admiration and adulation. By overlooking the aspects of their work that could be criticized and focusing on the things that can be praised, you will make your subordinates, superiors, and peers emotionally dependent on you for positive feedback.

"Boss, that was a great speech you gave before the Steam Rollers Local Twelve."

"Suzy, that was a great speech you wrote for the Boss to give before the Steam Rollers Local Twelve."

"Claudine, those were great shots your photographers took of the Boss giving his terrific speech before the Steam Rollers Local Twelve."

The recipients of this feedback will see you as a positive person, appreciative of their work activities. Despite whatever inner confidence in their own abilities they may possess, they still need outside reassurance from someone knowledgeable. You meet that qualification on the basis of your compliment. You have gained a "halo" effect, and you can do nothing wrong.

Negative Feedback: You may occasionally wish to change the behavior of a coworker. Resist the temptation to say, "I don't like the way you do this or that," or "Your work product is bad in this way or that," or "I think you spend too much time at the water cooler."

This approach creates anger and resentment rather than a behavioral change. It's about as effective as leaving anonymous graffiti on the wall behind the worker's desk.

Stage One in achieving a desired behavior change is to

point out similar undesirable behavior in a third party; for example, "Doesn't Harry spend a lot of time at the water cooler?"

If that ploy doesn't cut down on the worker's water-cooler time, switch to Stage Two, or the "five positive/one negative encapsulization." Give five positive statements or strokes, followed by a negative comment in the area you are attempting to change:

"Say, Bill, that was a hell of a good report you sent me last week. (One) Your area is becoming more productive than ever. (Two) The morale of your workers is extremely high. (Three) Everyone seems to be getting along. (Four) Things really seem to be operating smoothly there. (Five)"

If Bill doesn't say, "Will you please shut up and let me get a drink of water?" you move in with the negative stroke:

"Oh, by the way, Bill, would you do me a favor? Scuttlebutt has it there's a lot of loafing around the water cooler. I know it's necessary to get a break, but it looks bad."

Learn to say "I'm wrong" . . .

Another time to talk is when you've dropped the ball, made a mistake, or were obviously wrong in a statement or decision. If you admit the error and apologize for it, the chances of injury to your career are less than if you try to hide it from your peers or superior. Someone will find out and someone will tell. Admitting guilt on the gallows doesn't put the hangman out of a job.

"Boss, I'm sorry about my introduction of you last night. I meant to call you 'a great raconteur' instead of 'a great roué.' I looked up the words later, and I won't make the same error again."

If you admit your poor judgment or mistake quickly and openly, you may disarm a potential opponent seeking a long siege on your career over your error. In admitting your sin, you have disarmed him.

WHEN AND WHERE TO BITE YOUR TONGUE

Oscar Wilde wrote in *The Picture of Dorian Gray* about one of his characters, "He knew the precise psychological moment when to say nothing."

This enviable talent is worthy of cultivation. When not to talk includes what not to say. Aside from the rock-bottom immorality of gossip, it isn't in your best interests to become a contributing reporter to the company grapevine. If you suddenly learn that the Boss enjoys a Wednesday afternoon golf session, resist broadcasting the privacy. Spreading rumors, even true ones, is always inexpedient, and should be eschewed unless an action is seriously harmful to you or the company.

The old adage "If you can't say something good, don't say anything" is not just goody-goody advice. It is politically wise.

Say nothing in the staff meeting when the German-born sales manager, struggling with the English idiom to describe his success with a potential customer, explains that "the court is now in their ball."

Say nothing when one peer explodes about another peer and verbally rakes him with contempt for his incompetence, morals, and lust for junk food.

Say nothing of substance after you have had a few drinks. Lecturing the Boss over the punch bowl at the company Christmas party is not in the category of "clever business maneuvers."

Consider the general manager of a plant in Williamsport, Pennsylvania, who took his subcontract sales manager out for a fluid dinner the day they had hammered out a multimillion-dollar contract with a Big Three auto manufacturer. It was a joyous evening, and both bubbled happily over the day's accomplishment.

"You did a great job, Dorian," the GM said, "and I'll take care of you. Tell me, what job would you really like in the organization?"

Although Dorian's desire for advancement was natural and healthy, he should have held his tongue, but instead he said, "To tell you the truth, Boss, I'd like *your* job."

Bosses are allergic to such ambitions, and Dorian never again attained the same rapport with his boss, for soon after his demotion he left the company, a wiser and a broker man.

On certain occasions in our business lives, the words and actions of others call out for a response, an appropriate pun, a cry of anger, a sarcastic reference, or even a simple declarative sentence! But if the place or the person is inappropriate, wisdom decrees that we restrain our sallies and observations and supply of verbal arrows.

One executive who practices this restraint feels that bottling up his eloquent expletives is harmful to his health, so he vents his feelings and emotions at the commercials on television.

A quieter outlet is to invoke confidently the words of Robert Benchley:

Drawing on my fine command of language, I said nothing.

RULES FOR SILENCE

You win by not talking in the situations described above by simply not putting your foot in your mouth or your head on the block. Additional times not to talk are contained in the following Rules for Silence:

1. Don't Ask for Feedback

Asking for feedback on how you are doing is a sign of weakness. People intuitively feel that if you're confident and sure of what you are doing, you won't need feedback. Asking coworkers how they think you are doing your job gives them leadership over you. Control exists in their power to raise or lower you by stroking or not stroking.

To gain feedback from your subordinates, conclude each meeting with a brief critique—not to examine the work product, but the process. Comment on the way you think people have interacted, how they are feeling, and so on. Everyone at the meeting should be encouraged to do the same.

From such discussions you will not only gain information about a particular meeting, but you will acquire a general feeling of how you and others are doing without actively seeking their feedback.

Be cautious about setting up critiques among superiors and peers, however. Superiors could view it as "one of those newfangled ideas that promote worker participation on the job." Peers may see it as a game to catch them off guard.

2. *Withhold Positive Feedback*

The withholding of positive feedback is especially appropriate in the case of a subordinate who has been acting, even with good reason, as the king (or queen) of the department. He or she is looking for positive feedback and praise. The person is competent and has prepared a report for you, which you know he or she feels is particularly well done.

For your own good, take the subordinate down a peg: Accept the report; have him or her sit on the other side of the desk while you read it; then simply say, "Thank you," without further comment. You will witness the cockiness disappear—and it will reestablish the fact that he or she is one among many.

3. *Forget the Thank-you*

Suppose a peer has been giving you a difficult time over a mutual problem. At some point he or she tries to establish détente in the family by complimenting you on "that beautiful piece of work." Don't respond. Don't say a word. He will be more than a little uncomfortable in the pregnant pause that follows, and will know that you cannot be run over or influenced by compliments.

4. The "Never Mind, It's Hopeless Talking to You" Technique

The "Never Mind" carrot can be of inestimable value in an adversary situation. For example, you and a peer are at odds on the best position in The Company for one Scanlon Skinner.

You are of the opinion that "Scan," as he is nicknamed, should be offered a job in the microfilm department; your peer feels Scan should be sent to trade shows with his marketing department. You come to a confrontation. To disarm him, start a sentence that shows you intend to say something about him, "I feel that you, in the case of Scanlon . . ." and then stop, appear to change your mind, and say, ". . . Never mind."

Your peer will become anxious to know what it was that you were going to say and will want to pursue it. That night he will dream of how your sentence might have been completed.

This technique will quickly put you in control of your peer, and probably also Scanlon, who will be working in the microfilm department.

BEWARE OF THE PRESS

This warning does not translate as an order to your secretary to throw reporters out of the office; responsible journalists seeking legitimate stories are always welcome. It cautions against those journalists who—attempting to emulate Jack Anderson or Woodward and Bernstein—are seeking that odd angle, that slip of the tongue, that indefinable gaffe on your part that will plunge you into the headlines of the local paper, hit the wire services, and lead to embarrassment for you and your company.

Discretion calls for not talking to newspapermen/women, even "off the record," on a breaking story which could put your company in a controversial light:

Reporter: "Hi, there. You're spokesman for the Remarkable Vineyard Corporation, right?"

You: "That's right."

Reporter: "Well, an item just came over the wire that a vice-president of your company, Mr. A. Rexall Yorklip, was arrested last night for drunk driving in San Francisco. Do you have any comment?"

You: "Well, off the record, of course, that doesn't surprise me. There have been a number of occasions . . ."

Reporter: "Off the record, natch. Must be a real nuisance."

You: "Now don't get the wrong idea; you can't say a word about Mr. Yorklip—he's just been under a lot of pressure lately. And he's never been convicted of a thing! As for my official statement, you can say I'm sure it was all a mistake."

Reporter: "Right. How do you spell your name?"

You: "I don't want my name used."

Next day comes the story, and your big mouth has guaranteed that you can't do much about it:

> Mr. A. Rexall Yorklip, Vice-President of the Remarkable Vineyard Corporation, was arrested late last evening for driving under the influence of alcohol in San Francisco.
>
> A local spokesman for the company, who requested anonymity, confirmed that Mr. Yorklip had been arrested previously on similar charges but that police had been unable to obtain a conviction.
>
> The spokesman confided that Mr. Yorklip had been under a lot of pressure lately, but refused to disclose the reasons for this pressure.
>
> As a public service, this newspaper will begin tomorrow an in-depth series on Mr. Yorklip and the Remarkable Vineyard Corporation. We will explore all avenues to uncover the cause of his pressure.

The story about poor Yorklip above is a negative one.

But even if the story proposed about you and your company is positive, a magazine or newspaper puff piece could be harmful to the health of your career, mainly because of the "Great God Jealousy."

Even if you are featured in the media in a positive light and The Company can see its noble reflection in your eyes, the rampant jealousy of your peers and superiors may descend on your unwary carcass with flapping wings and eat away at your well-being and your future.

In summary . . .

Learning when to talk and when not to talk must be a consciously acquired political skill. If you acquire it, you will be far ahead in your race for business success. You will say what needs to be said when the proper occasion is at hand; you will be thoughtfully quiet when talk would halt or impede your progress. You will thank yourself that you have learned such skills.

> I have learned silence from the talkative, tolerance from the intolerant, and kindness from the unkind; yet, strange, I am ungrateful to those teachers.
>
> —KAHLIL GIBRAN

HOW TO LEAD:

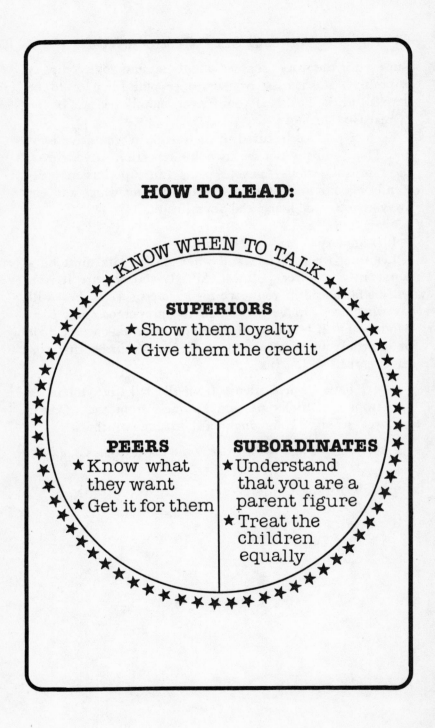

KNOW WHEN TO TALK

SUPERIORS
★ Show them loyalty
★ Give them the credit

PEERS
★ Know what they want
★ Get it for them

SUBORDINATES
★ Understand that you are a parent figure
★ Treat the children equally

Chapter 11. WHEN TO LISTEN

No man would listen to you talk if he didn't
know it was his turn next.

—EDGAR WATSON HOWE,
Ventures in Common Sense (1919)

In nearly every conversation, one party speaks and the
other waits for his turn to speak—the "me next" syndrome.
This is not to say that "me next" *hears* nothing; he may hear
just enough to trigger his own thoughts, on which he con-
centrates instead of *listening*.

Hearing and listening are different . . .

The subtle distinction between the two rests on *volition*.
While the words are often used interchangeably, *hearing*
refers more literally to the perception of sound through the
auditory sense, while *listening* involves the *act* of hearing
"with thoughtful attention" to understand the meaning of
the sound.

Hearing requires no effort; *listening* entails an effort to
perform the act. The rewards for increasing your efforts at
listening rather than just *hearing* may astound you.

LEVELS OF LISTENING

We are all occasionally guilty of various degrees of hearing without listening. But when we are hearing at only the

level of sound perception, oblivious to content, we may find ourselves in serious trouble.

Do your listening levels vary with the importance of the situation? Or with the potential danger—physical, social, professional—in not listening?

Picture yourself listening to the following people and try to imagine your listening level:

Your boss is outlining a proposal for a presentation you are to give in two days to the company's biggest client.

Your secretary is describing the bargains she found at a rummage sale on Saturday.

Your son is explaining how his team lost the soccer game.

Your boss is telling you about his vacation plans.

WHEN DO YOU LISTEN?

In the examples above, what motivated higher listening levels? The speaker? The subject matter? Fear? Love?

Did you picture yourself being distracted even when you wanted to listen?

Maintaining a high listening level may be difficult with dull subject matter, poorly presented material, or low-priority information. But can you afford not to listen?

When you confirm the importance of what someone has to say *by listening,* you're giving one of the most powerful forms of positive feedback. An additional benefit is the speaker's elevated estimation of your intelligence for recognizing the importance of what he says.

Most people have never learned how to listen . . .

Listening has recently gained noteworthy attention in industry, literature, and motion pictures. The advertisements of E. F. Hutton and the television messages of Sperry reflect the appreciation of this skill in the business community. Sperry, convinced that listening is an invaluable skill, have developed a system for employees to learn to listen.

Their course of instruction consists of tape presentations followed by actual listening exercises.

In the movie *Being There*, the late Peter Sellers, playing the part of an unknowledgeable oaf, convinces everyone he is very bright by keeping his mouth shut and appearing to listen attentively to everyone.

The protagonist in Shirley Hazzard's novel, *The Transit of Venus*, is described as a listener:

> Listening had been a large measure of her life: she listened closely—and since people are accustomed to being half-heard, her attention troubled them. They felt the inadequacy of what they said. In this way, she had a quieting effect on those about her, and stemmed gently the world's flow of unconsidered speech.

These illustrations all emphasize the powerful impact one can make by cultivating the generally neglected skill of listening.

LISTENING AS A POLITICAL TOOL

Learning to listen is the most important political tool you can have—a lifetime tool. Advice about being a "good listener" is usually met with indifference, but developing this rare political talent is of inestimable value.

It seems that *listening* should be, as Peter Sellers portrayed it, an easy talent to acquire. After all, it's not like learning to do something, is it? But perfection of this skill—like any other—requires practice to refine it and continued use to prevent its atrophy! Practice is what counts, as with most other human skills.

How do you become an expert listener? . . .

If you have until now been a talker instead of a listener, tell yourself that watching other people's behavior is an entertainment, a sport, a game. Remind yourself that "everyone has something to teach me, although it may not be what he or she thinks it is." What many people say may be meaningless and boring and untrue; but if you are actively engaged in observing their total behavior, you will not be bored. Watching people's behavior and what it says about them, and observing the total dynamics of how all those in the room interact, is endlessly fascinating. There is always something to learn when you act the invisible but observant mouse.

Turning the observation of other people into a sport, then, is the best way to learn to listen. Go to a meeting armed with the idea that whatever game other people are playing, you are in it for the sport of listening and observing behavior.

Try to develop as many devices and techniques as you can to help you listen and observe more effectively. Develop body-language gimmicks. Think up reminders to yourself. If your ego relies on clever comments which display your intelligence, keep reminding yourself that no matter how brilliant you may sound to yourself, you will be seen as an even brighter star by waiting until the strategically right moment . . . and then swooping in with the Twelve Words discussed in the previous chapter.

Begin developing your skills by playing detective at staff meetings. Pick someone to observe; and by listening carefully to all he says and noting his behavior, try to gain some insights about him. Consider Sam, for example, who talks a lot and makes jokes and tries to get everyone's attention.

The Boss has just entered the room for a staff meeting, and everyone stands at attention since he was once a military man and expects such fealty—everyone except Sam, that is. The Boss glares at him, and Sam slowly rises to his feet.

"Sorry, Boss," he says with a funny little smile on his face that says he doesn't mean it.

"That's okay," the Boss says, "I guess you have good reason to be tired." And everyone looks at Sam and wonders what the reason is.

As an exercise to develop your perceptive abilities, you might mentally interview the other staff members as to why they think Sam was too tired to get on his feet when the Boss came in.

There is a story in every person, and a mini-series in most encounters between two people. Be assured that even your wildest imagination is not likely to match the excitement of reality.

WINNING THE SPEAKER'S TRUST

Learning the skill of listening is only half the job of being a good listener. Once you have squelched and quieted your own noise, you must then evoke in the speaker a desire to talk. And that speaking must be of significance and purpose, as opposed to a cursory or vapid conversational exchange.

For the speaker to consider your listening a positive experience:

1. *He must have a high level of trust in you.*
2. *He must have the conviction you are sincerely interested in hearing what he has to say.*

A speaker develops trust in a listener only after he has confided in him without being criticized or hurt by what he has said. When he becomes so secure that their conversations will not be repeated to him through the garble of the grapevine, he will speak openly. At this trust level, the speaker, who has given you leadership in your relationship, will be supportive of your endeavors.

The second aspect of creating a positive listening experience for the speaker is the artistic challenge. Conveying a sincere interest in the speaker's subject can be achieved through "the art of facilitating a meaningful conversation." This art consists of:

1. *Active listening;*
2. *Passive listening;*
3. *The ability to begin conversations . . . "door openers."*

FACILITATING

A. Active Listening

Verbal Feedback

An active listener verbally assures the speaker that he understands; he restates his impression of what the speaker has said.

1. *Talker:* I don't know how to handle this unusual problem.
   Listener: We've never had one like this before.
2. *Talker:* We didn't accomplish anything today.
   Listener: You didn't like the meeting.
3. *Talker:* Why can't I get accurate reports?
   Listener: Errors make you angry.

Body Language

Active listening includes physical signs that show you are attentive. Demonstrate that you don't intend to talk while the other person is talking, except for the reassuring words and phrases noted above. You can do this with body language that signals your position and intention: For example, fold your hands and put them in front of your mouth while looking directly at the person. This sends the message, quite literally, that nothing is about to come out of your mouth. It says, "You're on. It's your turn, and I'm going to listen to you."

Salesmanship

Active listening is such a valuable tool that it has become the nucleus in the development of a new sales technique where the salesman does more listening and less talking to get better results.

Ordinarily the salesman does about 70 percent of the talking during a sales presentation, and the prospect does 30 percent. This may capture the prospect's attention and enthusiasm, but it rarely draws out that rational state of mind in which the client can make a serious decision.

Although the prospect may want a product or service, he is not likely to act until he feels he has a rational basis for decision.

The new sales technique is designed to satisfy the rational mature state of mind. The percentages of talking and listening are reversed; the prospect talks about 70 percent of the time, and the salesman limits himself to 30 percent. Ideally the salesman listens to the prospect until he discovers why the potential buyer needs his product or service. He next quotes the price and then the services offered, and concludes with a concise reclosing, or after-sell.

Active listening is generally considered the most valuable form of listening and will probably be your tool of choice most of the time. If you find that someone to whom you are listening is uncomfortable with this active approach, however, you can reduce your role to one of passive listening.

B. Passive Listening

Silence or a minimum response is often sufficient to encourage a speaker to pursue the natural inclination to talk. A good listener shows he is paying attention without disrupting or questioning the narrative flow. He may use gently encouraging body language, such as:

1. Nodding (in affirmation, not off to sleep);
2. Eye contact;
3. A chuckle;
4. A sympathetic sigh;
5. A low whistle;
6. An appreciative guffaw.

You can use unobtrusive words or phrases when the speaker seems to seek feedback:

7. "I see." (You might not, but say you do.)
8. "Yes," or "Yes?"
9. "Oh," or "Oh?" or "Oh!"
10. "Wow!"
11. "What do you think?"
12. "I understand."

You can repeat the last few words when the speaker stops talking:

> *Speaker:* "I went downtown yesterday . . ."
> *Listener:* ". . . yesterday. . . ."
> *Speaker:* "I'm convinced he's undermining morale. . . ."
> *Listener:* ". . . undermining. . . ."

Using the passive listening technique, you encourage the speaker to continue talking. When he hesitates, you reach over and give his accelerator a barely discernible tap.

When your intended speaker fails to open up to you spontaneously, a few key words may unlock his tongue. It pays to develop a few of these "door openers."

C. *"Door Openers" to Begin Conversations*

The business associate in search of a trusted and sympathetic listener may be just bursting to brag, feed you a problem, seek your understanding, or solicit your advice. All he or she needs is that little nudge. You can tell by the furrowed brow, the cat-ate-the-canary look, or the beseeching "Bless me, Father" that he or she is ready for confession.

Depending on the subject, which you are wise to ascertain before unlocking Pandora's box, select a key and gently turn:

1. "Can I help?"
2. "Tell me about it."

3. "Let's talk it over."
4. "Perhaps I can help you."

Once you coax the incipient speaker into a comfortable track, you can utilize either passive or active listening.

> *Important Disclaimer: All benefits from preceding rules are null and void if you try to fake it . . .*

Simply stated, if you don't feel like listening, don't.

D. How to Quash Conversation

Tell the person anxious for an audience that you'll talk later at a more appropriate time. Use any excuse: You have a headache, you're waiting for a call, you're on your way to a meeting. Otherwise it will be apparent that your heart is not in a conversation at the moment.

E. The Art of Acceptant Listening

The art of acceptant listening is to allow the speaker freedom to talk without fear of adverse judgments or rejection.

The counterpoint to this is nonacceptant listening, or, in the vernacular, turnoffs.

Dr. Thomas Gordon, a clinical psychologist and management consultant, cites twelve "Roadblocks" to communication, or conversation-stoppers, in his book, *L.E.T.*:

1. *Ordering, Directing, Commanding*
   You must do this.
   I expect you to do this.
   Go apologize to her.
2. *Warning, Admonishing, Threatening*
   You had better do this, or else . . .
   If you don't do this, then . . .
   You had better not try that.
3. *Moralizing, Preaching, Imploring*
   You should do this.

It is your responsibility to do this.
I wish you could do this.

4. *Advising, Giving Suggestions or Solutions*
What I think you should do is . . .
Why not take a different approach?
The best solution is . . .

5. *Persuading with Logic, Lecturing, Arguing*
Do you realize that . . .
The facts are in favor of . . .
Experience tells us that . . .

6. *Judging, Criticizing, Disagreeing, Blaming*
You are not thinking straight.
You didn't do it right.
That is a stupid thing to say.

7. *Praising, Agreeing, Evaluating Positively, Buttering-up*
You usually have very good judgment.
You have so much potential.
You've made quite a bit of progress.

8. *Name-calling, Ridiculing, Shaming*
You are a fuzzy thinker.
You're talking like an engineer.
You really goofed on this one!

9. *Interpreting, Analyzing, Diagnosing*
You're saying this because you're angry.
What you really need is . . .
You have problems with authority.

10. *Reassuring, Sympathizing, Consoling, Supporting*
You'll feel different tomorrow.
Behind every cloud there's a silver lining.
It's not that bad.

11. *Probing, Questioning, Interrogating*
Why did you do that?
How long have you felt this way?
Have you consulted with anyone?

12.   *Distracting, Diverting, Kidding*
      Think about the positive side.
      That reminds me of the time when . . .
      You think you've got problems!

Learn to listen to the New Boy in Town, the Grumblers,
and the Little People . . .

These are not the names of new Tolkien characters, but
neglected resources for useful company information.

1.   The New Boy in Town

Worlds of information can be gathered from a new employee. After his or her first few weeks with the company,
issue an invitation for an informal chat:

"You've been with the company for several weeks now,
Ann (or Aaron), and I would like your candid and honest
opinion of what you have found right and what you have
found wrong with the company. I value your judgment,
especially before you become completely brainwashed about
the importance of doing things the way they've been done
for ninety-two years. I'm aware that you're still a little over-
whelmed by the company's one-sided orientation, but before your individuality wears off and you become a company
clone, please tell me what you feel is obviously wrong, stupid,
unnecessary, out of line. . . ."

Ordinarily superiors and peers spend substantial amounts
of time defending a company's practices and policies to newcomers. They want to be sure everyone knows that the
status quo is *the* way of doing things. When a regulation or
procedure is questioned, the newcomer is assured that its
logic will be apparent when he has obtained more information.

If, instead, you listen to the newcomers, you'll have an
opportunity to see your systems and procedures through
unclouded eyes. Many organizational practices are obsolete

or should be terminated. The reasons for the practice may be a long-forgotten part of the organization's past and no longer germane.

It usually takes four to six months before a newcomer is completely integrated and no longer useful as a resource to question the validity of certain systems, procedures, and methods. During that virgin period, the new employee is a valuable asset. He should be listened to early because he is unique and his uniqueness will soon be lost.

2. *The Grumblers*

Have you ever heard that when the movie script calls for sound effects of an unhappy mob, the extras are told to chant "rhubarb, rhubarb?" The sound tells the sensible listener that the natives are restless.

Phil Mark wasn't a good listener. He thought his workers were saying "rhubarb."

While Phil was in college, he decided to pick up some extra cash by answering a Santa Claus ad in the local newspaper. With his rotund figure and a hearty "Ho, ho, ho," Phil walked away with the job and became a terrific Santa. He soon discovered there was a shortage of reliable Santas.

He developed the idea of hiring and training Santas, and supplying the finished product to department stores and nearby shopping centers. The first few years, he hired his fraternity brothers. Then he opened a Santa Claus school, began to make deals, and in a few years cornered the Santa Claus market in his area.

He quickly branched out into Easter bunnies, magicians, Mickey Mouses, and Donald Ducks. It was only logical to supply decorations to go along with his characters at Christmas and Easter and for other promotions. Phil Mark Enterprises grew dramatically. Phil became known nationwide in the shopping-center promotion business for his originality.

But Phil failed to listen—either to the grumbles of his workers or to the advice of some of his key associates. Employees tried to get his attention with legitimate complaints about working conditions, benefits, and his failure to communicate with them. His entrepreneurial style, although greatly successful in the marketplace, was causing a great deal of resentment among his workers. They felt isolated and grumbled that no one cared about them and their problems. They began to talk about unionization. Phil paid no attention; in desperation, one of the employees thought up a disruptive form of sabotage.

Phil's company had acquired as customers almost every major shopping center, and each had some specialized type of Christmas decoration and promotion. Phil Mark Enterprises would start to assemble the characters and build the decorations a year in advance.

Decorations were built on a mass-production basis, and as each shopping center's decorations were completed, they were placed in large, identifiable bins. Come September, the precut forms and decorations were shipped to the shopping centers, where they would be assembled at the appropriate time in November.

In retaliation against their neglectful employer, the employees conceived the idea of mixing up the bins. When they finished their dirty work, a shopping center from the midwest, for example, which had ordered a Santa, a reindeer, and a snowflake scene, would now receive three reindeer, a Santa head on the body of Snow White, and a caroling youngster who belonged in Texas. Every order was scrambled! Phil, as always, ran short of time and ordered the decorations shipped without any preshipment check-out.

When he arrived at his first customer (one of literally hundreds around the country), he discovered to his chagrin what had happened. There wasn't time to find and reroute the correct decorations; he couldn't tell what was missing, and if he knew, he couldn't locate it.

Most of the shopping centers and department stores made other local arrangements in a hurry; no one paid, and Phil's company suffered a major setback from which it took years to recover. Had Phil Mark listened to the Grumblers, they wouldn't have had to command his attention so dramatically. He's learned the hard way that if he wants to keep on hanging tinsel, he'll have to listen to Santa's helpers.

3. *The Little People*

We tend to listen to people of "importance" more intently, giving great weight to their advice simply because of their fame or the string of initials after their names. We may be disregarding the wisdom of some practical *little people* who have information we need to make a decision.

A typical example is the school custodian, usually not recognized as one of the most knowledgeable people in the school system. Those who are in a position to watch others unobtrusively often make the most profound observations.

The best way to illustrate this point is with the story of Selma, a restaurant hostess. One evening in 1951, Selma paid a visit to her cousins, whose successful family business prompted their search for a new lucrative growth business. The father and three brothers had already sought the advice of college professors, successful friends, and other experts on which business to enter.

During the evening, the conversation turned to viable business ventures. Selma quickly replied that based on her observations in the restaurant, her first choice for a business of her own would be loans and credit cards.

None of the college-educated young men took her seriously at first, but they asked her reasons.

"Simple," Selma replied. "People in the finance business arrive earliest 'or lunch at the restaurant; they stay the longest, order the most expensive items on the menu, and leave the biggest tips."

Suddenly ears and interest perked up. Selma was saying that people in the finance business had time to relax. Considering the time spent at meals, the type of meals ordered, and the generosity of their tips, business must be good . . . and without pressure! Maybe there was still not too much competition! The next day they ran a thorough check on the finance business in the area. It was not a business their advisers had recommended, but Selma was right.

Six months later, they opened their own finance company. Ten years after that, they sold the business for nearly $5 million. The best resource for the idea of going into the finance business was not someone well known or successful, but the restaurant hostess who could recognize success in her customers. Selma was one of those knowledgeable *little people*.

LISTENING FOR THE TRUTH

Our stress in this chapter has been on the art and skill of listening in the business sector. Listening does not, of course, imply that you believe, approve, or blindly trust every word you hear.

Good listeners cultivate a filtration system to separate the treasurable nuggets from verbal malarkey.

In organizational life never naïvely accept all you are told. Within any company there are those ostensibly selfless employers who stress their interest in your—and the company's—welfare. Don't believe a word of it.

With a little practice you can learn to identify some classic forms of the selfless, dedicated employer.

1. Listening to Superiors

The stark truth is that *there is little or no security at the executive level of any organization*. Whatever you have done in the past to promote your superior's or the company's interests is well-nigh forgotten. What have you done lately? Or what will you do in the near future? How can you help your superior look good in the eyes of his or her superiors?

You can hear pacifiers like the following and still find yourself with a pink slip if you don't continually deliver:

"The company thinks you are important and so do I."

"The company and I are most interested in your welfare."

"I'm only staying here to take care of my people—like you."

"I'll take good care of you." (He or she isn't kidding!)

"I get job offers all the time for more money, but turn them down because we have such a great company."

"You shouldn't take that job with the X company for more money, because there is more opportunity here. Just to show you that we really care about you, we'll pay you a thousand dollars more than they are offering you."

One specific time *not to listen* to your boss is when he says, "Come to the company seminar. We'll have a few drinks, fool around a little at night. Maybe we'll play some cards. And talk." You are momentarily tempted to believe that if you relax, you will be rewarded; but, in truth, you will be judged and evaluated, and your behavior will be observed and discussed in your superior's inner circle. And they are not about to let a stranger join the blessed ranks.

If you do have to go (and an invitation from your superior is sometimes tantamount to a command), don't drink too much. Forget your primitive fears that Prohibition is coming back. If you do succumb to all that free sauce, you may be seen as having a drinking problem, or say something you ordinarily wouldn't say: "Just between you and me, our president is a real turkey!" Drink a little beer or Dubonnet and soda (the dark red, as it looks stronger than it is), and you will be considered one of the boys.

At this same seminar, avoid the late-night poker game. You will be tired the next day and therefore less sharp. Remember that you are on trial. So play a little while and then go to bed. Use any excuse: The wife is calling; your father is failing; your mother is lonely; your feet are killing you; or you have a headache. You will be in a strange, lonely bed and out of your normal routine and will have sat more than your normal dosage. It may be hard to sleep, so give yourself every chance. A mild sleeping pill may not be a bad idea.

Because others will be observing and listening to you, be on time for meals or sessions; watch Monday night football even if you hate the game; find time after the sessions and in the morning for exercise in order to sleep better and be sharper.

2. *Listening to Peers*

If there is a fire in the skyscraper, everyone on the roof wants to get on the express elevator. If there is one job opening on the floor above you and your peers, there will be a mad and vicious scramble for this position. Maybe all should not be fair in love, war, and organizational life, but that's the way it is.

Because of your arena of combat, it is well to cultivate a keen, though not obvious, distrust of your peers. That means that you cannot trust their strategic flatteries, such as:

"I really like you."

"Let's stick together."

"You're my friend."

"Let's have lunch like this more often."

3. *Listening to Subordinates*

They think that flattery, as well as good work, will get them somewhere. They owe the continuance of their job security to you. Even if you are—as many bosses are—a bit of a bastard, you may hear the following paeans to your greatness:

"I stay here because of you."

'You're the only one around here I'll listen to."

"You're the only one around I would work for."

"I'd quit this job in a minute if it weren't for you."

"This place would fall apart if it weren't for you."

4. *Listening to Consultants, Accountants, and Lawyers*

Outside consultants, accounting firms, and attorneys des-

perately want the new contract and are willing to say and
do almost anything to get it. But this is what you hear:

"We stand on our integrity."

"We are proud of our independence."

"Impartiality is our middle name."

"We will take your account, but only if we know we can
do a superior job."

Some outside service organizations try to land a contract
by *telling the client what they think he or she wants to hear*
rather than the truth about a situation. There are, of course,
many excellent outside resources that can and often should
be used. Just don't be swayed in the selection process by
high-sounding words. Choose only after checking references
and examining previous work done.

5. *Listening to the Company Line*

The following story is about organizational deceit. It illustrates more graphically than any hypothesized situation
the importance of *listening* carefully to company statements
without always believing them. The management of an organization may be deceitful for its own ends, and you, the
employee, may suffer for it.

Shortly after you drive into Sikorsky Memorial Airport in
Stratford, Connecticut, if you look to your left, you will see
a reconstructed Marine Corsair, tethered tightly to its ce-
ment monument, dedicated in 1971 to Chance Vought, Inc.
Rescued from a military junkyard, this symbolic Corsair,
whose winged clones were once the mainstay of the economy
of Stratford and the surrounding Bridgeport area, now has
few admirers.

Occasionally, on a sunny Sunday a grandfather who had
worked at Vought as a child takes his grandson to see the
plane—the Navy's proud 400-mph warplane. It was the
fastest shipboard fighter in the world. Pilot heroes returned
from the Pacific to praise its performance in battle. In a

telegram to the Chance Vought employees in May 1943, Admiral Chester Nimitz wrote:

"Day to day fighting in the South Pacific has proven the Corsair decidedly superior to the Jap [then the accepted ethnic terminology] Zero. Our Naval and Marine pilots at Guadalcanal are enthusiastic about this plane which so regularly turns out a first rate job. Congratulations to all Chance Vought personnel on this outstanding contribution to the war effort. The Navy needs more planes to constantly increase the pressure on the enemy. Keep the Corsairs coming!"

The Stratford workers kept them coming. According to the Navy, Corsairs shot down 2,140 enemy planes, while only 189 of these planes were lost. In celebration of the thirtieth birthday of Chance Vought in 1947, a daylong air show and "open house" took place at the plant, and more than 20,000 people came to hail this vital part of Stratford's life and economy. By 1948, employment reached 8,500, with an annual payroll of over $20,000,000.

According to an article by George Sessions Perry in a June 1949 issue of *The Saturday Evening Post*, "It was the Navy in the autumn of 1946 [a year before the thirtieth birthday celebration] which 'urged' Chance Vought to move out of an area that in time of war might well receive the highest target priority of any section of the nation, since it is more productive, congested and accessible than most."

Perry concluded his article:

"As other vital companies take up the march to the havens behind the mountains, Chance Vought will remain a pioneer."

After the "urging" by the Navy in 1946, Chance Vought, "one of its largest purveyors of warplanes," sent a secret task force to look at and evaluate an empty 1,900,000-square-foot plant in Grand Prairie, near Dallas. North American Aviation had used the plant during the war, and employed 40,000 people. When the group returned, they dictated the foregone conclusion that the move was "feasible." *The deception had begun.*

Except for the task force and a few key executives, the Chance Vought organizational family was told nothing about plans in progress; but the children began to suspect that all was not right with their paternal leaders. Rumors of a possible pullout were circulating widely in the area.

On March 11, 1947, a spokesman for Chance Vought, in a public relations ploy to dissipate the smoke of concern, issued the following falsely reassuring statement:

"The company is not going to move to Texas despite reports that have been current for a year that it plans to. The company's position is that it will not move to Dallas— or anywhere else."

Just a year later, in April 1948, the official announcement was made that Chance Vought was going to move to Texas— lock, stock, and pork barrel.

By July 1949, the Stratford plant was an empty shell. Shipped to Texas. Also relocated to Chance Vought's new home were approximately 1,300 executives and skilled workers, leaving 7,200 individuals out of jobs in Stratford. Many of those who relocated later returned from Texas, disgusted and disillusioned with the company.

The editor of *The Stratford News* sought out Governor Chester Bowles to learn what had really happened. Was it the length of the runways? Was it the threat of atomic disaster? Governor Bowles said the answer was much simpler: The Navy had been told, he alleged, by a high-ranking politician from the Lone Star State that there were more votes in the House of Representatives from Texas than there were from Connecticut. And the Navy needed all the votes it could get in battling for funds with the Air Force, recently separated from the Army as a new branch of the military.

In 1949, the year of the move, Connecticut had eight congressmen; Texas had thirty-two congressmen.

Chance Vought, Inc., is now a division of the L.T.V.

Corporation, a conglomerate in which the "V" represents old Chance Vought.

In summary . . .

Learning to listen is the most important political tool.

This chapter helps you to focus on ways to improve your listening skills, and shows how to use those skills to improve your life in and out of the corporate world.

In order to listen effectively, one must recognize the conscious act of will involved as well as the tendency to listen at various levels in different situations. An ability to listen may be developed by concentrating on the game of listening to learn information.

Listening is further facilitated by developing "door openers" to begin conversations, along with techniques of active and passive listening to encourage different types of speakers.

Effective listening includes recognizing those from whom you can gain valuable information, and learning how to adjust your ear to compensate for the speaker's point of view.

Great rewards await those who learn to listen, for they will learn when and where to move, what to say, and how to achieve their wants.

HOW TO LEAD:

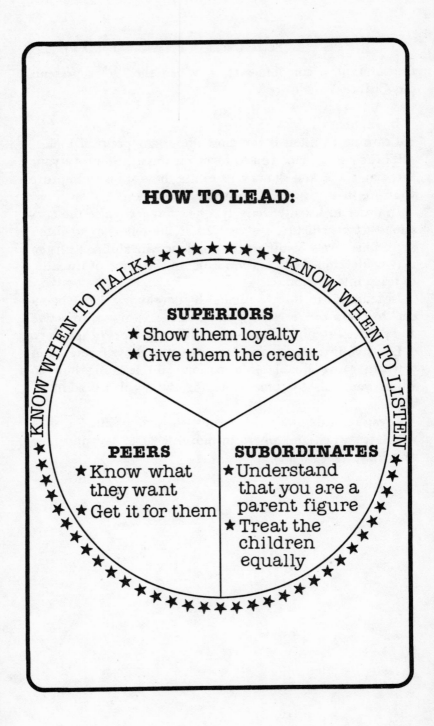

KNOW WHEN TO TALK ★ ★ ★ ★ ★ ★ ★ ★ ★ ★ ★ KNOW WHEN TO LISTEN

SUPERIORS
★ Show them loyalty
★ Give them the credit

PEERS
★ Know what they want
★ Get it for them

SUBORDINATES
★ Understand that you are a parent figure
★ Treat the children equally

Chapter 12. WHEN TO PUT IT IN WRITING

What is written without effort is, in general, read without pleasure.

—SAMUEL JOHNSON

Writing—like speaking—is most effective when the writer focuses on the intended recipient.

In the corporate arena, sensitivity to whether you are writing to your superiors, peers, or subordinates determines your political techniques.

When and when not to write to superiors

To develop a general rule on writing, observe your superior's style carefully to learn whether he or she responds better to material presented verbally or in written form. If you see a tendency in one direction or the other, act on it.

The competent manager, if not a fanatic word-hater, will expect written reports from you which convey where you are, what you are doing, and how things are proceeding. By submitting reports before deadline, you allow your superior time to read them. If they are also well done, the odds are good that your information or recommendations will be used in his decision making or meetings with his superiors.

It is useful to underline in red (or overline in yellow) the salient points of your report. In this way you can comfortably write as long and as detailed a report as necessary to cover all aspects of the subject (which reflects positively on your ability and thoroughness) while at the same time permitting your superior to skim and study only the summary points you have highlighted.

When interacting with a new superior, you should test how he or she prefers to relate. Although many expect regular written reports, others abhor receiving or sending anything in writing. Between the report-lovers and the report-haters are as many kinds of bosses as Heinz has varieties. Tune yourself to play in the same key as your superior. Learn to interact with him in a way that makes him feel comfortable with you. That's politics.

One way to determine if your superior likes or doesn't like to receive reports in writing is to examine his own written output. Is he a compulsive scrivener, or does he save his cache of terse statements for special occasions like promotions and organizational realignments and the like?

You can tell whether or not he reads your reports by the way he does—or doesn't—respond to them. If he writes a commendatory reply or a short observation on one of the points in the report, he has undoubtedly read it and you're on his beam: "I liked your plan to develop Building Site C before Building Site B, Ingelman. You had that in paragraph twelve, subsection c."

If he meets you in the hall and says, "I received your report, Finwhistle, but I don't know when I'll get a chance to read it," you're in a different ball game. If you hear nothing, it could be he doesn't like memos, the report is lost, or he can't read. If I were you, I'd opt for the fact he doesn't like writing.

If he or she doesn't like to interact in writing, the solution is simple: Avoid sending written material. It probably won't be read. You'll be frustrated. Your boss will become uncomfortable and maybe even feel guilty for not reading what you write. Wisdom is not making your boss feel guilty.

Everyone avoids people around whom they feel guilty, and the easiest way for a boss to avoid you is—you guessed it—fire you!

Never write politically sensitive material to a superior. If there has been a miscue in the department, don't be the one to document it so his or her adversaries can get a copy of the document and use it as a tool to cause embarrassment.

If the boss likes detail, then narrate as full a story as possible. If he or she favors tightness, then hand in the condensed version.

The word *mogul* has various definitions. *Moguls* are defined here as wheeler-dealers with an aversion to receiving or sending anything in writing. Most do, eventually, learn to read the provisions of bankruptcy law.

An apparently successful company president asked me to perform a confidential study of a possible acquisition for his company. The targeted business was in Europe, and I spent three weeks on the Continent, talking to key people, traveling, entertaining, probing, visiting government offices; and then I spent another week at my New York office refining my fifty-page report. Naturally I included a detailed but concise summary.

I sent him a copy of the report together with a hefty bill. At our meeting the following week, he greeted me, "I received your report, but I haven't read it. What does it say?" He wanted a two-minute oral summary and not a substantive written report on which he could act intelligently.

Is it any wonder that Mr. Empty Files—who, I quickly learned, abhorred the written word—was totally disorganized and lacked a single employee who knew what was going on, what had passed, or what was planned? Here was a company, probably the largest of its kind in the world at that time, unquestionably the largest in this country, whose president chose to emulate the ostrich, stick his head in the sand, and ruminate in blind solitude.

Mass confusion pervaded the organization: The managers

received no leadership or direction, and they were neither encouraged *nor allowed* to submit reports on the progress and problems of their divisions and departments.

Mr. Files had no possible way of knowing the direction in which the company was headed—downhill—since he refused to look at anything written about it. Capable managers, aware of the necessity for reports and for documentation, soon followed the siren song of the headhunter to other companies.

This ship of fools, once so promising with its inspired launching, size, and quality of personnel, soon rammed into the shoals of bankruptcy. The small band of hip-shooting wheeler-dealers who had remained with the company were still firing wildly at unlikely targets as the ship went down. It would have been better if they had kept the company log.

Unhappy employees of organizations whose superiors are distrustful of the written word—and probably jealous and suspicious of anyone who can produce an intelligent memo or report—are wise to go along with the information blackout long enough to put their résumés in the mail.

When and when not to write to subordinates

The general rule on writing to subordinates is: *do it almost always*. It seems that the more written communication a superior has with his or her subordinates the better the organization runs. The superior who takes the time and the effort to write subordinates' performance reviews, set their goals, and give directions is better understood and, therefore, gets better results.

As a superior, you are the role model for your team. If your communications are short, concise, tight, and exact, your subordinates will respond accordingly—as they will if your messages are sloppy or ambiguous.

On December 20, Jasmueller, you wrote that by May

1st, the roof of the cafeteria would be completely reno-vated. Today is May 2nd, and I don't buy your excuse that you can't fix the roof when it's raining and you can't tell where the leaks are when it isn't raining. You have a week to get the tar on or the hell out.

Jasmueller will certainly respond.

As a superior, promote the rule within the organization that "if it isn't written, it didn't happen."

This, of course, means that any unrecorded action re-ceives no credit at the time of the performance evaluation or review. How often have you heard, "I really didn't say *that*, I said such and such," and the listener responds. "No, I'm sure you didn't say such and such. You said *that*"? And back and forth it goes. This generates fudging and blame-throwing, and is automatically corrected with the installa-tion of written communications.

Writing also provides an opportunity to clarify your think-ing on a subject. As Francis Bacon wrote, "Reading maketh a full man, conference a ready man, and writing an exact man."

A written statement seems to carry more weight than a verbal one. The written document sits firmly in your file, fraught with promises and deadlines, and is hard to argue with. The very act of writing turns an idea into a commit-ment; an agreement into a contract which must be fulfilled.

New educational techniques require students to sign written contracts with their schools, determining their ac-complishments during the year. Students who sign such con-tracts appear to achieve substantially more education than those who do not. Evidence indicates that contracting stu-dents set high initial goals and then stretch to meet those lofty targets. Teachers more often find students setting goals unattainably high than trying to slide by with minimally low ones.

A woeful tale of not writing . . . an expensive mistake

The marketing procedure of a small, successful credit-card company involved purchasing the private accounts of local stores to increase credit-card customers. A women's department store which agreed to sell its accounts to the company had accumulated a number of "clinkers"—customers who couldn't or wouldn't pay.

After reviewing the list of newly acquired accounts and crossing off the names of those whose credit was bad or questionable, the credit-card company sent the list to a manufacturer who embossed the cards and mailed them directly to the customers.

In a few days, armed with their shiny new credit cards, customers of all kinds were taking to the stores, and the cash registers were ringing—but not for the credit-card company! It seems an employee had sent the embosser a nice, clean list without any names crossed off.

Well, the simplest and most obvious goat was the employee who sent out the list—but was he or she to blame? Had this employee been given written instructions regarding the appropriate list to send?

As surely as the compass points north, the arrow of accountability ultimately points to the top executives of the company. In the case of the employee, the superior erred twice. First, he had given verbal directions rather than written ones. Second, he didn't check to see if his oral instructions had been followed. As far as written procedure was concerned, he erred again in not creating an official, *new*, typewritten list of the cardholders—*sans* the credit risks.

Although the rule of record is to *write* to your subordinates, the appropriate communication is sometimes a verbal one. Dictating a letter for your secretary to type is poor style if the matter is personal in nature. When a subordinate experiences a death or a birth or a marriage, etc., he or she wants your human contact and your response as a human being. A handwritten note may be in order, but personal contact should also be arranged.

Verbal interaction is always called for when a subordinate is being fired. It's simply humane to help the person being dismissed to deal with the trauma such an event causes. You, as the superior, are in the best position to explain why this thing has happened, and anyone who is being let go has a right to know. Such information helps prevent similar results on suceeding jobs and will ease the shock. Your experience as well as your personal contact may help an employee through this difficult time. To be fired without acknowledgment by the superior is humiliating.

Write to peers—as little as possible

When dealing with peers, avoid writing whenever possible. Your painstaking reports will find themselves in the rotary file or the thresher. If you come across as less than illustrious or as the company "wit" (half- or otherwise), rest assured your words will be efficiently reproduced and brought to the attention of the party or parties unknown who will clip your wings and damage your image and ambition.

If you fear accusations of inefficiency for your reluctance to write to peers regarding joint projects, then write you must. Such mutual projects seem fairly rare in the everyday workplace, however.

But if—in these written communications—you infer any negative assessment of your peers' operation and organization, you will have created lifelong enemies who will be fighting—not assisting—your advancement.

To summarize the questions of when to write and when not to write, we evoke the classic answer of "yes," "no," and "maybe": subordinates—generally "yes"; peers—generally "no"; and superiors—"maybe."

Writing as a logical and political tool

Following are some effective ways to use writing as a logical and political tool.

Business Letters: Start really *looking* at them before they are mailed. And take a good, hard look at some of your company's recent correspondence. Does it reflect the image you want to project? Is the grammar questionable? Are there spelling errors or typos or noticeable corrections? Is the letter laid out attractively on the page in an acceptable business form?

Even good secretaries forget basic rules from time to time. Buy your company a good book on business letters and grammar. Then buy a superior grade of stationery. The impact of your letters—positively or negatively—cannot be overestimated. And it is one of the simplest areas to refine.

Memos: A copy of the memo should be sent to anyone mentioned in the text. Avoid blind copies; they show up mysteriously at the most inopportune moments. Don't set deadlines in writing that are not real deadlines. You'll soon be branded as the boy or girl who cries wolf.

A memorandum whose impact is potentially equivalent to the H-bomb ends as follows:

". . . If I don't hear from you to the contrary by 5 P.M. on August 5, I will, of course, proceed as stated above."

Such memos are both a threat and an insult. If they are somehow lost and go unread, the sender could proceed on a personal course of action, oblivious to serious objections.

Personal Notes: Don't overlook the little friendly note. Its informality can take the sharp edge off of a particularly touchy relationship.

Forms: Although valuable time-savers within your own team, forms can turn off outsiders quickly. Especially avoid those smudgy forms with carbon paper bearing the heading "A Memo From _____."

Meetings: When you call a meeting, create and distribute the agenda beforehand. Have minutes taken, but be sure to edit them. All too often something politically damaging appears in meeting minutes.

Formal Written "Position Papers": When dealing with an

important issue, it is often worthwhile to prepare a "position paper." Instead of tossing your ideas out at a meeting in the hope that everyone will catch and write them down, clarify and formalize your thoughts on paper.

A quick way to produce a quality position statement is to invite a bright and trusted colleague to listen to your explanation of the material while you record it on tape. Encourage the listener to ask any questions until you are sure he or she understands the ideas you are trying to impart Have the tape transcribed, editing out the questions and any redundancies. Without a great deal of effort, a clear "position paper" will emerge. These papers are an impressive political tool too rarely utilized in business.

The Press: Being published at the appropriate time and place can put you in a good light politically. Many organizations are impressed with employees who write, particularly articles of relevance to their company.

A distinction must be made between the publicitymonger previously mentioned and the published writer, whose expertise gains him credibility.

You don't have to join the ubiquitous "Corporation of the Goosequill," as William Thackeray labeled the profession of journalism, to get your words and thoughts and ideas in print. If you write well and have original ideas, you should be able to find a market for your articles. The company newsletter is one outlet; trade magazines serving your industry are another; the specialty publications which cover your profession are a third.

In general

The pen is the tongue of the mind.
—MIGUEL DE CERVANTES

We must not take Cervantes too literally. The mind does not coat its perceptions with flowery words, phrases twisted with adjectives and adverbs, or needlessly modified and mutilated sentences in the name of literary expression. But let the owner of that same laconic mind take pen to hand, and watch out! That small phallic symbol seems to take on a life of its own! And that life all too often seems spawned in Renaissance England rather than Spartan Greece.

The tendency to embellish the written word can obstruct a reader's comprehension of even the most brilliant concepts. A solution to such belabored and ostentatious epistles is offered by the writer Sydney Smith:

> In composing, as a general rule, run your pen through every other word you have written: you have no idea what vigor it will give your style.

In summary . . .

The importance of writing as a political tool is generally underrated in the business community, where functionalism seemingly precludes attention to the art.

Professional success can be greatly affected, however, by sensitivity to a superior's desire for or distrust of written reports, a subordinate's need for written clarification and direction regarding performance and goals, or a peer's resentment of your literary efforts.

Awareness of the intended recipient's position enables you to form guidelines for your written matter, whether it be a business letter, office memo, or personal note. The politically wise also consider the impact on all possible readers of such apparently innocuous material as forms, meeting minutes, and formal position papers.

Whether your writing undermines your effectiveness in other areas or serves you as a powerfully effective political tool depends on the attention you give to the form, the substance, and the decision to write at all.

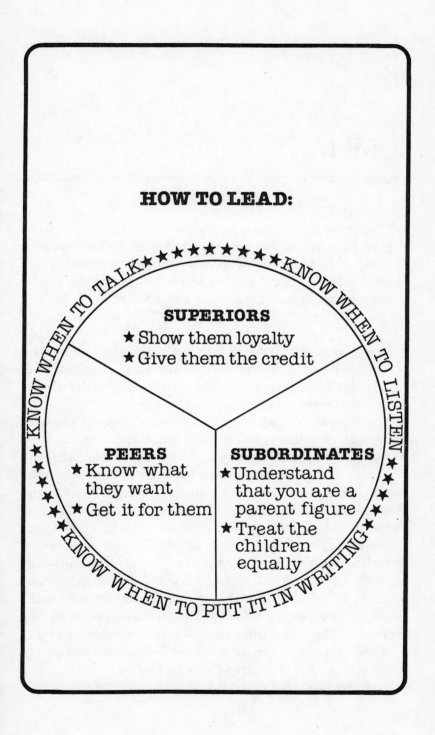

HOW TO LEAD:

★ KNOW WHEN TO TALK ★ ★ ★ ★ ★ ★ ★ ★ ★ KNOW WHEN TO LISTEN ★ ★ KNOW WHEN TO PUT IT IN WRITING ★

SUPERIORS
★ Show them loyalty
★ Give them the credit

PEERS
★ Know what they want
★ Get it for them

SUBORDINATES
★ Understand that you are a parent figure
★ Treat the children equally

SUMMARY

> If a man has a talent and cannot use it, he has failed.
> If he has a talent and uses only half of it, he has partly
> failed. If he has a talent, and learns somehow to use the
> whole of it, he has gloriously succeeded, and won a sat-
> isfaction and a triumph few men ever know.
>
> —THOMAS WOLFE

How effectively one handles the processes and interactions
of the work world determines whether work is primarily a
joyous and satisfying experience utilizing one's talents or a
source of frustration and overwhelming conflicts.

These processes and interactions include logical management skills as well as political skills. Much attention has been
devoted to methods for developing logical management
skills, but little serious emphasis has been placed on the development of interactional or political skills. While it might
seem that greater management skills would decrease the need
for political skills, quite the reverse is true. The highest performers often develop the most adversaries, and their career
growth and salaries rarely reflect their accomplishments—unless they add political leadership skills to their logical management abilities. A sensible career game plan includes both.

Logical skills, at the base of successful management, should
establish a clean structure, employee participation, goal setting and performance reviews, time management, and procedures for decision making and problem solving.

Any organizational work involves interactions with supe-

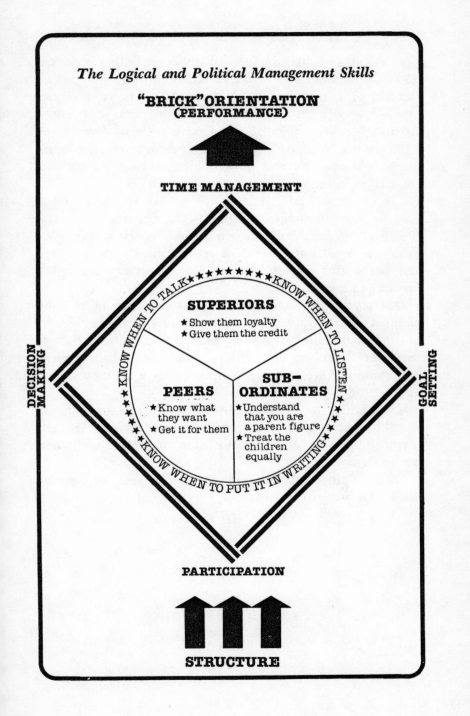

The Logical and Political Management Skills

"BRICK" ORIENTATION
(PERFORMANCE)

TIME MANAGEMENT

DECISION MAKING

GOAL SETTING

KNOW WHEN TO TALK ★ ★ ★ ★ ★ ★ ★ ★ KNOW WHEN TO LISTEN

SUPERIORS
★ Show them loyalty
★ Give them the credit

PEERS
★ Know what they want
★ Get it for them

SUB-ORDINATES
★ Understand that you are a parent figure
★ Treat the children equally

KNOW WHEN TO PUT IT IN WRITING

PARTICIPATION

STRUCTURE

riors, peers, and subordinates. Even the head of an organization is accountable to someone: a board of directors, a parent company, a governmental agency, stockholders. A clear picture of the political realities within an organization is essential to the development of an effective personal game plan. This requires a thorough analysis of these interactions, the company's structure and philosophies, and your goals and current position in relation to all of the above.

The ability to lead is generally thought of as a skill needed only by those in charge of others. To the politically aware, the ability to lead—to influence to some conclusion or condition—is equally important in relationships with superiors and peers. Anyone can develop this leadership ability by learning and practicing specific techniques.

One leads a superior with loyalty and by giving him the credit. One leads subordinates by setting a good example, by dealing as individually and equitably with them as though they were members of a family, and by establishing clear expectations. One leads peers by learning what they want— and getting it for them.

Tools which facilitate the effective operation of both political leadership skills and logical management skills include learning when to talk, when to listen, and when and when not to write.

Contrary to popular sentiments, political realism is not at odds with integrity.

ABOUT THE AUTHOR

Raymond Blank heads R. M. Blank Associates, a multi-discipline consulting company. He specializes in consulting, and conducts seminars in management and organizational development, business strategies, and research.

Before entering the consulting field, Mr. Blank founded a company which grew to an annual volume of over $250 million. He has held management positions and served on the boards of directors of *Fortune* 500 companies.

Mr. Blank has been honored for his consulting work by the U.S. Department of State, as well as by foreign governments and by agencies. He received a commendation from the Governor of Maryland for his efforts in restructuring education in that state, and won the Seklemian Advertising Award in 1970.

Mr. Blank has structured recent graduate-level Harvard Business School case studies. In addition to his business education, Raymond Blank holds a doctorate of law.